QUESTIONS AND ANSWERS
ON THE DUTIES OF
ESOP FIDUCIARIES

Questions and Answers
on the Duties of
ESOP Fiduciaries

David Ackerman

The National Center for Employee Ownership
Oakland, California

This publication is designed to provide accurate and authoritative information in regard to the subject matter covered. It is sold with the understanding that the publisher is not engaged in rendering legal, accounting, or other professional service. If legal advice or other expert assistance is required, the services of a competent professional person should be sought.

Legal, accounting, and other rules affecting business often change. Before making decisions based on the information you find here or in any publication from any publisher, you should ascertain what changes might have occurred and what changes might be forthcoming. The NCEO's Web site (including the members-only area) and newsletter for members provide regular updates on these changes. If you have any questions or concerns about a particular issue, check with your professional advisor or, if you are an NCEO member, call or email us.

Questions and Answers on the Duties of ESOP Fiduciaries
David Ackerman
Book design by Scott S. Rodrick

Copyright © 2008 by The National Center for Employee Ownership. All rights reserved. Printed in the United States of America. No part of this book may be reproduced or transmitted in any form or by any means, electronic or mechanical, including photocopying, recording, or by any information storage and retrieval system, without prior written permission from the publisher.

The National Center for Employee Ownership
1736 Franklin Street, 8th Floor
Oakland, CA 94612
(510) 208-1300
(510) 272-9510 (fax)
Web site: www.nceo.org

ISBN: 1-932924-48-5
ISBN-13: 978-1-932924-48-0

Contents

Foreword xv
By Corey Rosen, NCEO Executive Director

Chapter 1: Determining Fiduciary Status

Q1	Who is a fiduciary?	2
Q2	Does a person's title or function govern fiduciary status?	3
Q3	What types of activities will typically render a person a fiduciary of a plan under ERISA?	4
Q4	What types of offices or positions result in fiduciary status?	4
Q5	When can a person be a fiduciary only for a limited purpose?	5
Q6	Can a person ever be a fiduciary if the person does not perform one or more of the fiduciary functions described in Section 3(21)(A) of ERISA?	6
Q7	What is a named fiduciary?	7
Q8	What are the duties of a named fiduciary?	7
Q9	What is the purpose of having a named fiduciary?	8
Q10	How are named fiduciaries designated in the plan document?	9
Q11	Can the liability of a named fiduciary be delegated?	9
Q12	Who selects the named fiduciaries?	9
Q13	What are the considerations that should be taken into account in appointing the named fiduciaries?	10
Q14	What is an ESOP trustee?	12
Q15	What is a directed trustee?	12
Q16	Is the plan sponsor a fiduciary?	18
Q17	Are members of a plan sponsor's board of directors plan fiduciaries?	19
Q18	Can individuals who are officers or employees of a plan sponsor be plan fiduciaries?	22

Q19	Can corporate officers and directors be plan fiduciaries for some purposes, but not for others?	23
Q20	What is the plan administrator?	24
Q21	Are plan administrators ESOP fiduciaries?	25
Q22	When are professional service providers considered plan fiduciaries?	25
Q23	If a professional service provider who is a member of a professional firm renders services to a plan in a fiduciary capacity, can the other members of the professional firm be considered fiduciaries?	27
Q24	When can an in-house professional service provider be considered a plan fiduciary?	27
Q25	May other plan fiduciaries serve as professional service providers?	28

Chapter 2: Fiduciary Duties

General 31

| Q26 | What are the primary fiduciary duties under ERISA? | 31 |

The Exclusive Benefit Rule 32

Q27	What is required for a fiduciary to satisfy the "exclusive benefit" requirement?	32
Q28	Is it a violation of the exclusive benefit requirement if the fiduciary's action also benefits the employer?	34
Q29	If officers or directors of the plan sponsor also serve as plan fiduciaries, can they be held liable for business decisions that adversely affect the value of stock held by the ESOP?	35
Q30	May ESOP fiduciaries take into account whether a proposed transaction will preserve employment for plan participants?	36
Q31	May ESOP trustees vote themselves on to the plan sponsor's board of directors?	37
Q32	Does ERISA prohibit a bank from serving simultaneously as an ESOP trustee and as a lender to the plan sponsor?	39
Q33	Can an ESOP fiduciary be held liable for misrepresenting facts regarding the plan or the plan sponsor?	40

Contents | vii

Q34	Can an ESOP fiduciary be held liable for withholding material information regarding the plan sponsor? 41
Q35	Does an employer have a duty to disclose information about proposed changes to an ESOP? 44
Q36	Must an ESOP fiduciary turn over a copy of the valuation report to a participant who requests to see it? 44

The Prudence Standard 45

Q37	What must a fiduciary do to satisfy the prudence requirement?........45
Q38	What is the legal standard for determining whether a fiduciary's acts are prudent? 45
Q39	Are a fiduciary's actions judged by the standard of an ordinary person or that of an expert? 46
Q40	What other standards do courts employ in determining whether an ESOP fiduciary has satisfied the prudence requirement? 46
Q41	How does the prudence requirement apply with respect to voting stock of the sponsoring employer? 47
Q42	Should an ESOP fiduciary monitor or seek to influence the management of the plan sponsor? 47
Q43	How does the prudence requirement apply with respect to forecasting an ESOP company's repurchase obligation? 49
Q44	What role should an ESOP fiduciary play in determining the appropriateness of executive compensation? 51
Q45	Can an ESOP fiduciary avoid liability for an imprudent decision by establishing that he or she acted in good faith? 53
Q46	What is the standard of review applied by courts in evaluating the prudence of the conduct of an independent ESOP fiduciary?.....53
Q47	What is the standard of review applied by courts in evaluating the prudence of the conduct of an ESOP fiduciary who has a conflict of interest? 54
Q48	What is the difference between "substantive prudence" and "procedural prudence"? 55
Q49	What constitutes procedural prudence?..56
Q50	Does an ESOP fiduciary have an obligation to seek the assistance of an expert to satisfy the prudence requirement?.........................60

Q51	Will an ESOP fiduciary be absolved of liability if he or she acts in reliance upon the advice of a qualified independent adviser?..............60
Q52	Can a trustee be held liable for an imprudent resignation? 61

Diversification 63

Q53	What is required for a fiduciary to satisfy the ERISA diversification requirement?...63
Q54	If an ESOP holds assets in addition to employer stock, do the diversification rules apply?..63
Q55	Are there any other circumstances under which an ESOP fiduciary has a duty to diversify plan assets?...64
Q56	What are the primary factors for prudent diversification?...................69

Following Plan Documents..69

Q57	What is required for a fiduciary to discharge his or her responsibilities in accordance with plan documents?...................................69
Q58	What is pass-through voting? 70
Q59	If the plan document provides for pass-through voting, is the ESOP trustee obligated to follow voting directions that he or she receives from plan participants and beneficiaries?..........................70
Q60	Can there be circumstances under which an ESOP fiduciary must disregard voting directions from plan participants and beneficiaries even though the plan document provides for pass-through voting?...71
Q61	What procedures should an ESOP trustee follow in soliciting voting instructions? 72
Q62	What specific actions should an ESOP trustee take to ensure that pass-through voting is conducted on a free and fair basis? 72
Q63	What is "mirror voting"?..73
Q64	Are ESOP trustees required to comply with mirror-voting provisions? 73
Q65	May an ESOP plan document grant to plan participants the authority to direct the trustee with regard to tendering of stock allocated to their accounts in response to a tender offer? 74
Q66	If the plan document provides that any offer to purchase shares of the plan sponsor must be passed through to the participants, must the ESOP trustee always follow the participants' directions?....75

Q67	What action should an ESOP trustee take to ensure that participants' directions regarding response to a tender offer are proper?...76
Q68	What is "mirror tendering"?...76
Q69	Are mirror-tendering provisions in ESOP plan documents valid?........77

Chapter 3: Prohibited Transactions

Q70	What is a prohibited transaction?..82
Q71	Are there any statutory exceptions to the prohibited-transaction provisions?...83
Q72	Are payments made to ESOP participants in satisfaction of their rights to benefits under the plan subject to the prohibited-transaction rules?...84
Q73	May a plan fiduciary receive a benefit from the plan?....................85
Q74	May a person serve as a plan fiduciary if he or she is involved in a different capacity with a party in interest?...................................85
Q75	Who is a party in interest or a disqualified person with respect to a plan?...85
Q76	What are the differences between the prohibited-transaction rules under the Code and ERISA?...86
Q77	What plans are covered by the prohibited-transaction rules?.........87
Q78	When is a fiduciary liable for engaging in a prohibited transaction under ERISA and the Code?...87
Q79	What are the penalties for engaging in a prohibited transaction?.....88
Q80	Can a prohibited transaction be corrected?...................................89
Q81	Is the full excise tax imposed on each disqualified person who participates in a prohibited transaction?..89
Q82	May a plan purchase insurance to cover any losses to the plan resulting from a prohibited transaction?...90
Q83	What types of transactions are included in the prohibition against lending money or the extension of credit between a plan and a party in interest?...90
Q84	What is an exempt loan?...91
Q85	What are "qualifying employer securities"?...................................91

Q86 Under what circumstances are loans from a plan to participants and beneficiaries permissible?..92

Q87 May a party in interest ever furnish goods and services to a plan?...93

Q88 What is a "reasonable contract or arrangement" for furnishing goods, services, or facilities between a plan and a party in interest?...94

Q89 May a fiduciary who receives full-time pay from a sponsoring employer receive compensation for his or her services to a plan?......94

Q90 When may a fiduciary who receives full-time pay from a sponsoring employer receive reimbursement or advances for expenses incurred on behalf of the plan?..95

Q91 May plan expenses be paid out of the plan?..95

Chapter 4: Purchases and Sales of Employer Securities

Q92 Under what circumstances may an ESOP purchase or sell shares of the plan sponsor's stock from a party in interest?.................98

Q93 What does the term "adequate consideration" mean?..........................99

Q94 Has the Department of Labor published regulations interpreting the term "adequate consideration"?..99

Q95 What is a "generally recognized market" for a security?.......................99

Q96 How do the Department of Labor regulations define the term "adequate consideration"?..101

Q97 How is the term "fair market value" defined in the adequate consideration regulations?..102

Q98 What information should be contained in the written documentation of valuation?...103

Q99 What additional information is required in the written documentation of valuation where the asset being valued is a security for which there is no generally recognized market?...........104

Q100 In valuing employer securities for which there is no generally recognized market, may the existence of a "put" option be considered?...105

Q101 May an ESOP trustee pay a control premium for employer securities?..105

Q102	If an officer, director, or shareholder of the plan sponsor serves as the trustee, can the "control in fact" requirement be satisfied so as to justify the payment by the ESOP of a control premium for employer securities?	106
Q103	May an ESOP trustee pay a control premium for a minority interest combined with an option to purchase sufficient additional shares to constitute a controlling interest?	106
Q104	What steps should an ESOP trustee take to justify paying a control premium for a minority interest combined with a right to purchase sufficient additional shares to obtain control?	107
Q105	Are there other considerations to take into account in evaluating a "creeping control" transaction?	108
Q106	How is the "good faith" component of the adequate consideration test interpreted?	110
Q107	What must an ESOP fiduciary do to satisfy the Department of Labor that he or she has acted in good faith?	116
Q108	What are the relevant criteria for determining whether an appraiser is independent?	117
Q109	May ESOP appraisals be performed by the accountants for the plan sponsor?	119
Q110	To what extent is an ESOP trustee entitled to rely upon a valuation prepared by an independent appraiser?	119
Q111	What methods should an ESOP fiduciary employ to investigate a proposed purchase of employer securities?	124
Q112	What matters should an ESOP fiduciary direct legal counsel to investigate in connection with a proposed stock purchase?	127
Q113	Should an ESOP fiduciary become involved in contract negotiations in connection with a proposed stock purchase?	129
Q114	What additional considerations should an ESOP fiduciary take into account in a multi-investor transaction?	129
Q115	Under what circumstances may an ESOP trustee sell stock of the plan sponsor?	130
Q116	If an ESOP trustee receives an offer to purchase stock of the plan sponsor at a price in excess of the appraised value of the stock, must the stock be sold?	132

Chapter 5: Personal Liability

Q117 Can a fiduciary be held personally liable for a breach of duty? 134

Q118 Is a fiduciary liable for a breach not occurring during the fiduciary's term in office? 134

Q119 Is there a duty to remedy a fiduciary breach committed by a predecessor fiduciary? 135

Q120 What types of remedies can be imposed on a fiduciary for a breach of fiduciary duty? 136

Q121 What losses may a fiduciary be liable to restore? 137

Q122 What is the measure of a plan's loss to be restored as a remedy for a fiduciary breach? 137

Q123 Can any gains offset a loss resulting from a fiduciary's breach? 139

Q124 What profits may a fiduciary be liable to give up? 139

Q125 What types of equitable remedies have been applied in ESOP cases? 139

Q126 What is the 20% penalty for breach of fiduciary duty? 141

Q127 What excise taxes and other penalties may apply to a fiduciary breach? 141

Q128 May a fiduciary face criminal liability for a breach of fiduciary duty? 142

Q129 Are there other laws imposing criminal liability on a fiduciary? 142

Q130 Do any federal crimes specifically apply to employee benefit plans? 142

Q131 May a fiduciary face civil liability for interference with rights protected under ERISA? 143

Chapter 6: Protecting Against the Risk of Liability

Q132 May a plan release a fiduciary from liability? 146

Q133 May a fiduciary be relieved from his or her fiduciary duties by delegating duties with respect to a plan to another individual? 147

Q134 May a plan fiduciary indemnify its employees who actually perform the fiduciary services for the plan? 147

Q135 May a plan purchase insurance for itself or for plan fiduciaries to cover liabilities or losses resulting from the acts or omissions of plan fiduciaries? 147

Q136	May a fiduciary or an employer purchase insurance for the plan fiduciary to cover liability or losses resulting from the acts or omissions of the plan fiduciary?	148
Q137	What losses are covered by a typical fiduciary liability insurance policy?	148
Q138	Who is typically covered under a fiduciary liability insurance policy?	149
Q139	What is the difference between an ERISA bond, employee benefits liability insurance, and fiduciary liability insurance?	149
Q140	What policy limits are appropriate?	149
Q141	May an employer who sponsors an ESOP indemnify a fiduciary?	149
Q142	May a plan reimburse a fiduciary's legal expenses incurred in defending a lawsuit charging breach of fiduciary duties?	151
Q143	If a fiduciary is found liable for breaching his or her fiduciary duties, can the fiduciary be held liable for attorneys' fees?	151
Q144	May attorneys' fees be recovered by a defendant in an ERISA action?	152

About the Author 153

About the NCEO 155

Foreword

In an age of litigation, acting as an ESOP fiduciary can be a scary proposition. After all, fiduciaries are held personally responsible for acts that cause losses to the plan in a way that violates plan documents or the law. Although corporate indemnification and insurance are likely (if not entirely certain) to cover most or all of that, the pain of having to go through lengthy court proceedings can be considerable. Being a fiduciary is also a demanding task that requires a considerable amount of time to keep up with changes in the law or plan documents, making decisions on valuation, voting ESOP shares, responding to offers for the company, dealing with participant concerns, and many other matters.

But fiduciaries should also take heart. While the responsibilities are indeed serious, if they do their homework, hire good advisors, and strive to act in the best interests of plan participants, the chances of being sued at all, much less being sued successfully, are extremely small.

Compared to other benefit plans, ESOPs have a very good record for staying out of court. Over their more than 30-year history, perhaps 20,000 ESOPs have been formed (about half eventually were terminated for one reason or another, most often because of a sale at a good price to another company). Yet fewer than 300 lawsuits have made it to court. Most litigation revolves around improper valuation, while the remainder most often results from differences of interpretation as to how the plan is or should be operated in terms of distribution policies. A variety of other issues, such as improper allocations, tax disputes, excessive executive pay, and incorrect vesting rules, are raised only occasionally. A quick perusal of the suits that have been litigated shows a high percentage involve companies or individuals whose behavior fails the "smell test." Most often, the actions of the company were so egregious that one must cheer for the plaintiffs and wonder how anyone thought the defendants could get away with what they tried. On the other hand, some suits are prompted by excessively aggressive plaintiff legal theories that stand no chance of winning (but cause a lot of aggravation). Finally, some suits result from simple ignorance or misinformation rather than ill intent.

Who Is a Fiduciary?

Under ERISA, those filling certain roles are designated as "named fiduciaries." Normally, plan trustees are named fiduciaries because they make fiduciary decisions and are named in the plan document as the fiduciary. However, anyone who makes decisions or causes someone else to make decisions concerning plan assets is a fiduciary, no matter what title they may have. So a board has certain fiduciary duties simply for appointing and monitoring a trustee, as well as when it directs a trustee to make a decision, for instance. Providing the trustee false or misleading information that will be used to make decisions can also make the provider a fiduciary.

About 83% of closely held companies have inside fiduciaries, who often are officers of the company. While sellers can be fiduciaries (in fact, anyone can be a fiduciary), it creates a clear conflict of interest that should be avoided. Most public company ESOPs, as well as about 17% of closely held company ESOPs, have outside fiduciaries. Some of these are directed trustees, but most are independent. Directed trustees have minimal fiduciary obligations; instead, these obligations are passed on to those giving them the directions. Having an independent trustee, while adding costs, also provides a layer of protection in terms of assuring courts, employees, and government agencies that the ESOP is not being run for interests primarily outside the ESOP.

There are a number of key fiduciary obligations, including to:

- *Act in best interests of plan participants:* The primary obligation of a fiduciary is to make sure decisions put the interests of participants, not other shareholders or the company, first.
- *Act prudently:* Fiduciaries need to be well informed and well advised in making responsible decisions for plan assets.
- *Follow the plan document:* It sounds obvious, but many fiduciary errors come from assuming, rather than knowing, what the plan says (and means).
- *Follow the law:* The law is a complex, ever-changing set of rules, regulations, court decisions, advisories, etc. Fiduciaries should keep informed through publications, conferences, Web sites, and other resources.

- *Diversify when required or necessary:* ESOP fiduciaries have more leeway on this than in other retirement plans, but it is not unlimited.
- *Make required filings:* A good plan administrator is the best resource to make sure this happens.
- *Pay only reasonable plan expenses:* There is government guidance on what expenses can be paid by the plan itself.
- *Obtain qualified counsel:* The NCEO can help you to locate advisors and give you general advice on what to look for.

Within these general obligations, there are several typical key fiduciary acts, including:

- *Assuring the ESOP pays not more than fair market value for the shares:* This is arguably the most important and complex matter fiduciaries must address. Remember that a good appraiser is just the start. The appraiser is simply an advisor to the plan, and the fiduciary ultimately must decide that the ESOP is paying not more than fair market value when buying from outside sellers and paying fair market value when buying back shares from participants.
- *Consider the effect of the repurchase obligation on value:* Far too many fiduciaries do not consider this, leading the plan to ignore a cost that may be well in excess of ordinary benefit costs.
- *Releveraging:* When an ESOP takes on new debt, the value of existing shares is affected negatively. In some cases, fiduciaries may want to try to mitigate that impact for employees nearing distributions, especially if they are near retirement age. Any such effort, of course, must not discriminate in favor of more highly paid employees.
- *Responding to offers to purchase the company or sell some of the ESOP's interest:* Fiduciaries must act in the best long-term interests of plan participants as shareholders, not as employees. But a higher offer price is not necessarily in participant interests if the ESOP can deliver greater value long-term.
- *Making acquisitions:* Buying other companies will have an impact on existing share value or distributions that needs to be considered.

This is not an issue of doing an acquisition or not but rather the way in which it is done.

- *Plan termination:* The board decides whether to terminate the plan (it is not a fiduciary decision), but the way in which termination is handled does have fiduciary implications for such issues as the proper allocation of unallocated shares, distributions, and vesting.
- *Executive compensation:* Fiduciaries must act as responsible shareholders. If executive compensation is excessive, this is a waste of corporate assets fiduciaries should object to.
- *Managing non-employer stock investments prudently:* Non-stock investments should be managed much as they would be in any other qualified retirement plan, not simply parked somewhere convenient.
- *Making sure the plan is operated in a nondiscriminatory fashion and that all plan requirements are followed:* Many plans allow for discretion in their operations, such as when distributions are made, but these decisions are fiduciary acts that must be made so as not to discriminate in favor of more highly paid people.
- *Corporate governance:* In their shareholder role, fiduciaries should act as responsible owners protecting the interest of participants.

While this is a broad outline of what fiduciaries do, there are many questions that arise in day-to-day practice. This book, written by one of America's foremost experts on ESOPs, provides an accessible and detailed look at the fiduciary questions that arise in an ESOP context. It can serve as a companion to the NCEO publication *The Inside ESOP Fiduciary Handbook,* a shorter narrative overview of fiduciary responsibilities (while *The Inside ESOP Fiduciary Handbook* is aimed at inside fiduciaries, novice independent fiduciaries may find it useful as well). Because no publication can ever be fully comprehensive or anticipate future changes, if you are an NCEO member, do not hesitate to contact us at the NCEO with any additional questions you may have.

Corey Rosen
National Center for Employee Ownership (NCEO)

CHAPTER 1

Determining Fiduciary Status

Contents

Q1	Who is a fiduciary?	2
Q2	Does a person's title or function govern fiduciary status?	3
Q3	What types of activities will typically render a person a fiduciary of a plan under ERISA?	4
Q4	What types of offices or positions result in fiduciary status?	4
Q5	When can a person be a fiduciary only for a limited purpose?	5
Q6	Can a person ever be a fiduciary if the person does not perform one or more of the fiduciary functions described in Section 3(21)(A) of ERISA?	6
Q7	What is a named fiduciary?	7
Q8	What are the duties of a named fiduciary?	7
Q9	What is the purpose of having a named fiduciary?	8
Q10	How are named fiduciaries designated in the plan document?	9
Q11	Can the liability of a named fiduciary be delegated?	9
Q12	Who selects the named fiduciaries?	9
Q13	What are the considerations that should be taken into account in appointing the named fiduciaries?	10
Q14	What is an ESOP trustee?	12
Q15	What is a directed trustee?	12
Q16	Is the plan sponsor a fiduciary?	18
Q17	Are members of a plan sponsor's board of directors plan fiduciaries?	19
Q18	Can individuals who are officers or employees of a plan sponsor be plan fiduciaries?	22

Q19	Can corporate officers and directors be plan fiduciaries for some purposes, but not for others?	23
Q20	What is the plan administrator?	24
Q21	Are plan administrators ESOP fiduciaries?	25
Q22	When are professional service providers considered plan fiduciaries?	25
Q23	If a professional service provider who is a member of a professional firm renders services to a plan in a fiduciary capacity, can the other members of the professional firm be considered fiduciaries?	27
Q24	When can an in-house professional service provider be considered a plan fiduciary?	27
Q25	May other plan fiduciaries serve as professional service providers?	28

Q1 Who is a fiduciary?

A fiduciary is defined by ERISA[1] as any person who, with respect to an employee benefit plan:

1. exercises any discretionary authority or control over the management of the plan;
2. exercises any authority or control over the management or disposition of the assets of the plan;
3. renders investment advice for a fee or other compensation with respect to plan funds or property; or
4. has any discretionary authority or responsibility regarding the administration of the plan.[2]

This definition generally includes plan trustees, plan administrators, members of plan investment or administrative committees, investment managers, and the persons who select or appoint other fiduciaries. The

---

1. The Employee Retirement Income Security Act of 1974 (ERISA), Public Law 93-406.
2. ERISA § 3(21)(A).

term "fiduciary" is intentionally broad so that the standard of conduct prescribed under ERISA applies to a broad range of individuals in order to hold them responsible for the misuse of plan assets, losses to the plan arising out of their violation of ERISA, or other wrongdoing relating to a plan. A person may become a fiduciary either by being named as a fiduciary in the plan document, pursuant to a procedure specified in the plan document, or by performing any of the fiduciary functions listed above.

Q2   Does a person's title or function govern fiduciary status?

Under the broad definition of "fiduciary" set forth in ERISA, fiduciary status is determined by the person's function rather than title.[3] If a person or entity has authority to exercise, or actually exercises, any of the functions described in Question 1, the person or entity will be deemed to be a fiduciary.[4] A person may be a fiduciary with respect to a plan for a limited purpose and also perform other, nonfiduciary roles with regard to the same plan.[5]

The term "fiduciary" can encompass plan sponsors, boards of directors of companies sponsoring employee benefits plans, plan committees, individual or institutional trustees, investment managers (which include registered investment advisors, banks, trust companies, and insurance carriers), administrative service providers, employees, consultants, attorneys, accountants, plan professionals, and plan employees (and each person who selects, appoints, and supervises or monitors the performance of any of these persons).[6] In particular, a plan committee appointed by the board of directors of the employer may very well constitute a fiduciary by reason of having discretion to act with respect to a plan. Moreover,

---

3. *Olson v. E. F. Hutton & Co., Inc.*, 957 F.2d 622, 625 (8th Cir. 1992).
4. *Confer v. Custom Eng'g Co.*, 952 F.2d 34, 40 (3d Cir. 1991); *Blatt v. Marshall and Lassman*, 812 F.2d 810, 812 (2d Cir. 1987); and *Eaves v. Penn*, 587 F.2d 453, 458 (10th Cir. 1978) (discussed in Question 125).
5. *John Hancock Mutual Life Ins. Co. v. Harris Trust and Savings Bank*, 510 U.S. 86 (1993); *Maniace v. Commerce Bank of Kansas City*, 40 F.3d 264, 267 (8th Cir. 1994).
6. DOL Reg. §§ 2509.75-5 and 2509.75-8.

the individual members of a committee are most likely fiduciaries if the committee itself is a fiduciary.[7]

Q3 What types of activities will typically render a person a fiduciary of a plan under ERISA?

Any activity performed by a person that is within the scope of the functions described in Question 1 will render that person a fiduciary with respect to the plan. Any person becomes a fiduciary if he or she performs (or has the authority or responsibility to perform) any activity relating to the management or administration of a plan or relating to the investment of plan assets. These activities include, for example:

- appointing other plan fiduciaries,
- delegating responsibility to or allocating duties among other plan fiduciaries,
- selecting and monitoring plan investment vehicles,
- acquiring or disposing of plan assets,
- interpreting plan provisions, and
- making decisions under the plan.

A person who only performs activities of a purely ministerial nature (such as calculating benefits, processing claims, and maintaining records) generally is not a fiduciary of a plan under ERISA. (See the discussion of purely ministerial acts that are not fiduciary in nature in Question 6.)

Q4 What types of offices or positions result in fiduciary status?

Some offices or positions with respect to an ESOP, by their very nature, require persons who hold them to perform one or more of the fiduciary functions described in Question 1. For example, a plan administrator of an ESOP, by the very nature of his or her position, must have discretion-

---

7. *See Martin v. Harline*, 15 EBC 1138 (D. Utah 1992) (individual member of the board of directors) (discussed in Question 17).

ary authority or discretionary responsibility in the administration of the plan. Plan administrators therefore are fiduciaries.

Other offices and positions should be examined, on a case-by-case basis, to determine whether they involve the performance of any of the functions described in Question 1. For example, an ESOP company might designate as a "benefit supervisor" an employee whose sole function is to calculate the amount of benefits to which each plan participant is entitled in accordance with a mathematical formula contained in the plan document. The benefit supervisor, after calculating the benefits, would then inform the plan administrator of the results of his or her calculations, and the plan administrator would authorize the payment of benefits to a particular plan participant. Since the benefit supervisor does not exercise any *discretionary* authority in performing the benefit computation, and does not perform any of the other functions described in Question 1, the benefit supervisor *would not* be a plan fiduciary.[8]

However, the plan might designate as a "benefit supervisor" a plan employee who has the final authority to authorize or disallow benefit payments in cases where a dispute exists as to the interpretation of plan provisions relating to eligibility for benefits. Under these circumstances, the benefit supervisor *would* be a plan fiduciary, since the benefit supervisor exercises discretionary authority in the administration of the plan and exercises control over the disposition of plan assets.[9]

Q5   When can a person be a fiduciary only for a limited purpose?

A person can be a fiduciary for a limited purpose only, such as having responsibility for managing a limited portion of the plan assets or for delegating fiduciary responsibility to another person.[10] For example, an investment manager might have responsibility for only that portion of the assets of an ESOP not invested in stock of the plan sponsor.

If the plan so provides, any person or group of persons may serve in more than one fiduciary capacity (including, for example, serving

---

8.   DOL Reg. § 2509.75-8, D-3.
9.   *Id.*
10. ERISA § 405(b); DOL Reg. § 2509.75-8, D-4.

both as trustee and administrator).[11] Fiduciary responsibilities that do not involve the management and control of plan assets may be allocated among named fiduciaries, and named fiduciaries may designate persons other than named fiduciaries to carry out fiduciary responsibilities (if the plan document expressly provides procedures for the allocation or designation). In these circumstances, the person delegating fiduciary responsibility to another has direct fiduciary responsibility only for the prudence of the initial delegation and for prudently monitoring the continued delegation.[12]

Q6 Can a person ever be a fiduciary if the person does not perform one or more of the fiduciary functions described in Section 3(21)(A) of ERISA?

Generally, no. Unless a person is a named fiduciary, the person will be a fiduciary only if he or she performs one or more of the fiduciary functions described in Section 3(21)(A) of ERISA, as set forth in Question 1. (See the discussion of named fiduciaries in Questions 7–13.) Persons performing purely ministerial functions within guidelines established by others are not plan fiduciaries. Department of Labor (DOL) regulations list the following functions as ministerial and, therefore, nonfiduciary in nature:

1. application of rules to determine eligibility for participation or benefits;
2. calculation of service and compensation for benefit purposes;
3. preparing communications to employees;
4. maintaining participants' service and employment records;
5. preparing reports required by government agencies;
6. calculating benefits;
7. explaining the plan to new participants and advising participants of their rights and options under the plan;

---

11. ERISA § 402(c)(1).
12. ERISA § 405; DOL Reg. § 2509.75-8, D-4, FR-12, & FR-16.

8. collecting contributions and applying them as specified in the plan;
9. preparing reports covering participants' benefits;
10. processing claims; and
11. making recommendations to others for decisions with respect to plan administration.[13]

Q7 What is a named fiduciary?

A named fiduciary is a fiduciary who is either named in the plan or identified pursuant to a procedure specified in the plan. Every plan is required to have at least one named fiduciary.[14] Examples of named fiduciaries are the persons serving as trustees, the plan administrator, and investment managers. Department of Labor regulations suggest that if a corporation is a named fiduciary, then the plan also should designate individuals by name or title to carry out specified fiduciary responsibilities under the plan.[15]

> *Planning Pointer.* If a plan sponsor follows the Department of Labor's suggestion, it should be careful not to inadvertently cause the individuals so named to become named fiduciaries. The functions of the individuals should be limited to specific functions, and their potential liability then will be limited to those functions. If the individuals are "named fiduciaries," then they will be personally liable for all phases of the operations of the plan. (See the discussion of the purpose of having a named fiduciary in Question 9.)

Q8 What are the duties of a named fiduciary?

A named fiduciary is jointly and severally responsible with co-fiduciaries for controlling and managing the operation and administration of a plan.

---

13. DOL Reg. § 2509.75-8, D-2; see *Flacche v. Sun Life Assurance Co. of Canada*, 958 F.2d 730 (6th Cir. 1992); *Demaio v. Cigna Corp.*, 16 EBC (BNA) 1627 (E.D. Pa. 1993); and *Reichling v. Continental Bank*, 813 F. Supp. 197 (E.D.N.Y. 1993).
14. ERISA § 402(a).
15. DOL Reg. § 2509.75-5, FR-3.

A named fiduciary must appoint trustees who have responsibility over plan assets, unless the plan document designates the trustees.[16] A named fiduciary also has the responsibility to hear benefit and claims appeals of participants and beneficiaries under the plan's claim procedures.[17] Plan documents may provide for the allocation of responsibilities among named fiduciaries and may authorize named fiduciaries to delegate non-trustee fiduciary responsibilities to others.[18] (See the discussion of delegation in Questions 11 and 133.)

Q9 What is the purpose of having a named fiduciary?

The purpose of designating a named fiduciary is to enable employees and other interested persons to ascertain who is responsible for operating the plan. The advantage of designating a named fiduciary is to focus liability for mismanagement with a measure of certainty by limiting the exposure to liability to that named person. Thus, in the absence of conduct that falls within the rules governing co-fiduciary liability, the liability of a fiduciary who is not a "named fiduciary" is generally limited to the functions that the fiduciary performs with respect to the plan; and the fiduciary will not be personally liable for all phases of the management and administration of the plan.[19] The Supreme Court has stated that ERISA is intended to focus liability on those actually responsible for operating a plan: "ERISA has eliminated . . . the common law's joint and several liability, for all direct and consequential damages suffered by the plan, on the part of persons who had no real power to control what the plan did."[20]

---

16. ERISA § 403(a).
17. ERISA § 503(2).
18. ERISA § 405(c)(1).
19. DOL Reg. § 2509.75-8, FR-16; *Birmingham v. SoGen-Swiss Int'l. Corp. Retirement Plan*, 718 F.2d 515, 521–522 (2d Cir. 1983).
20. *Mertens v. Hewitt Assocs.*, 508 U.S. 248 (1993) (actuary, as nonfiduciary, was not liable for damages as a result of knowing participation in a fiduciary breach).

Q10 How are named fiduciaries designated in the plan document?

The plan document should explicitly designate the plan's named fiduciaries.[21] However, the named-fiduciary requirement can also be satisfied without making specific reference to the term "named fiduciary." If the plan document clearly identifies one or more persons by name or title, combined with a statement that those persons have authority to control and manage the operation and administration of the plan, the requirement is satisfied. Thus, a plan document may provide that the plan committee (identified by name or title) will control and manage the operation and administration of the plan.[22]

Q11 Can the liability of a named fiduciary be delegated?

Yes. If responsibilities are prudently allocated among named fiduciaries according to plan procedures designed for that purpose, a named fiduciary will not be liable for the acts and omissions of other named fiduciaries, except as provided in ERISA's co-fiduciary rules.[23] Similarly, named fiduciaries will not be liable for the acts and omissions of a person who is not a named fiduciary in carrying out the responsibilities delegated to that person, provided that the named fiduciary prudently selects and monitors the actions of that individual.[24]

Q12 Who selects the named fiduciaries?

Typically, the plan sponsor selects the named fiduciaries. In addition, a named fiduciary may be chosen by another named fiduciary, by an employee organization with respect to the plan, or by the plan sponsor and employee organization acting together.[25] For example, a plan may permit

---

21. DOL Reg. § 2509.75-5, FR-1.
22. DOL Reg. § 2509.75-5, FR-1, FR-2.
23. DOL Reg. § 2509.75-8, FR-13. For further discussion of this point, see Question 126.
24. DOL Reg. § 2509.75-8, FR-15.
25. ERISA § 402(a).

the trustees to appoint one or more investment managers to control the management of the assets of the plan.[26]

Q13 What are the considerations that should be taken into account in appointing the named fiduciaries?

In naming a fiduciary, an employer or fiduciary should ensure that the named fiduciary meets the qualification requirements for a fiduciary under ERISA. A fiduciary can be an individual, partnership, corporation, joint venture, trust, estate, incorporated organization, association, or employee organization.[27] However, a person who has been convicted of certain crimes, including robbery, bribery, extortion, and fraud, is not permitted to serve as a fiduciary for a period of 13 years after the conviction or until the end of imprisonment for the crime, whichever is later.[28] In addition, an individual or organization may be temporarily or permanently restricted from serving as a fiduciary due to an "egregious breach" of fiduciary duty in the past.[29]

Because the laws establishing the standard of conduct for an ESOP fiduciary are complex (see Questions 26–69), plan sponsors and fiduciaries should take care to assure that persons named as fiduciaries with respect to their plans either are knowledgeable about the applicable fiduciary rules or have the willingness and capability to become knowledgeable about these rules. Once a person becomes a fiduciary, he or she is bound to follow the ERISA rules. Because the rules apply to a person immediately upon becoming a fiduciary, the fiduciary should understand the rules before becoming a fiduciary or, at the very latest, when he or she actually becomes a fiduciary. The law does not provide a grace period for a fiduciary to learn the applicable rules.

Because ERISA requires a fiduciary to discharge his or her duties solely in the interest of the participants in the plan and their beneficiaries,[30] in considering who should act as a fiduciary with respect to an

---

26. ERISA § 402(c)(3).
27. ERISA § 3(a)(9) and § 3(21)(A).
28. ERISA § 411(a).
29. ERISA § 409(a); see *Martin v. Feilen*, 965 F.2d 660 (8th Cir. 1992) (discussed in Question 27, Example 1).
30. ERISA § 404.

ESOP, the plan sponsor and other fiduciaries should evaluate potential conflicts of interest. An obvious conflict of interest is presented where the person designated to serve as trustee of the plan is a shareholder of the plan sponsor who will be selling shares of the plan sponsor to the ESOP. Officers and employees of the plan sponsor also may be presented with conflicts of interest when serving as ESOP fiduciaries. ERISA does not prohibit conflicts of interest and, in fact, it expressly authorizes officers and employees of a corporation to serve as trustees of employee benefit plans sponsored by their corporation.[31] However, fiduciaries with conflicts of interest are required to subordinate their personal interests to the interests of the participants in the plan. Persons responsible for designating ESOP fiduciaries should consider whether proposed fiduciaries will be able to function with complete loyalty to participants in the plan and, in this regard, they should take into account the fact that courts generally will accord a high degree of deference to the decisions made by independent trustees, while subjecting the actions of conflicted trustees to strict scrutiny. See Questions 46 and 47. For a further discussion of conflicts of interest, see Questions 27–32.

> ***Planning Pointer.*** When an individual is appointed as a fiduciary (or as a member of a plan committee that is a fiduciary), the new fiduciary should be made aware that he or she is assuming fiduciary functions, with the risk of personal liability for a breach of fiduciary duty. In addition, plan sponsors should educate fiduciaries and potential fiduciaries (such as members of the board of directors) as to their roles and responsibilities with respect to the ESOP. The fiduciaries should also be made generally aware of any fiduciary insurance coverage that has been provided and limitations on that coverage. For a discussion of fiduciary insurance, see Questions 136-140. The person or entity appointing the new fiduciary may wish to furnish this information in writing at the time of appointment and obtain a written acknowledgment from the new fiduciary.

---

31. ERISA § 408(c)(3).

Q14   What is an ESOP trustee?

ERISA requires that every employee benefit plan must have one or more trustees, who are named in the plan document or are appointed by another named fiduciary.[32] The trustees must have *exclusive* authority and discretion over the management and control of the assets of the plan, except in two instances. First, the trustees may be subject to the *proper* directions of another named fiduciary that are made in accordance with the terms of the plan and that are not contrary to the provisions of ERISA.[33] In that case, the trustee is called a "directed trustee." Second, the authority to manage, acquire, or dispose of assets of the plan may be delegated by the trustee or another fiduciary to an investment manager.[34] To ensure that the persons who act as trustees recognize their special responsibilities with respect to plan assets, trustees must accept appointment before they act as trustees.[35]

Q15   What is a directed trustee?

The trustee of an ESOP, by definition, always will be a "fiduciary" under ERISA as a result of his or her authority or control over plan assets. However, not all trustees have the same authority or discretion to manage or control the assets of a plan. ERISA specifically recognizes that a trustee will have limited authority or discretion when he or she is subject to the directions of another named fiduciary who is not a trustee, such as the plan administrator, the plan sponsor, an investment manager, or the participants in the plan.[36] A trustee who is subject to the direction of another named fiduciary is commonly referred to as a "directed trustee." The responsibilities and potential liability of a directed fiduciary will be reduced to the extent that his or her responsibilities are properly delegated to another fiduciary.[37] However, the trustee must determine that directions

---

32. ERISA § 403(a).
33. ERISA § 403(a)(1).
34. ERISA § 403(a)(2).
35. ERISA § 403(a).
36. ERISA, § 403(a).
37. ERISA, § 405(c); *Ershick v. United Missouri Bank of Kansas City, N.A.*, 948 F. 2d 660 (10th Cir. 1991) (holding that ESOP trustee, acting at the specific

that he or she follows are proper, are made in accordance with the terms of the plan, and are not contrary to the provisions of ERISA.[38]

It is difficult to define the scope of a directed trustee's responsibilities with precision. Although one federal court of appeals has held that a directed trustee is not a fiduciary,[39] the courts generally have found that a directed trustee retains fiduciary responsibility, even though modified and lessened.[40] In this regard, the court in the *Enron* case noted that, under ERISA, the named fiduciary who directs the trustee must not itself be a trustee and that the named fiduciary does *not* become a "directing trustee"

---

direction of the plan administrator to purchase additional company stock despite its diminishing value, was not liable for breach of fiduciary duty absent evidence that the trustee used its position for its personal benefit to the detriment of the participants) (discussed in Question 46). *See also Newton v. Van Otterloo*, 756 F. Supp. 1121 (N.D. Ind. 1991) (directed trustee did not breach his fiduciary duties because he lacked actual knowledge that the members of the ESOP committee, which had directed him to abstain from voting, had conflicts of interest and had not performed a proper investigation of their options in voting unallocated shares of stock and thus had breached their fiduciary duties) (discussed in Question 31, Example 2).

38. ERISA, § 403(a).
39. *Maniace v. Commerce Bank of Kansas City, N.A.*, 40 F.3d 264 (8th Cir. 1994). That case involved a company that had converted a profit sharing plan into an ESOP. Under the terms of the ESOP plan document, the board of directors of the plan sponsor appointed an administrative committee that was given a broad grant of powers and was specifically designated both as the "named fiduciary" and as the "plan administrator." The trust agreement provided that the trustee would be subject to direction by the committee with respect to the purchase, sale, or retention of company stock. Throughout the 1980s, the sales, net worth, and profits of the company generally declined. The company declared bankruptcy in 1989, and the employer stock held in the ESOP became worthless. The trustee took an essentially hands-off approach to the business problems encountered by the company and resigned as trustee in 1988. Plan participants sued the trustee, alleging that it had failed to fulfill its fiduciary obligations to prudently manage and protect the plan assets. The court held that the trustee was not a fiduciary with respect to the company stock because it had no discretion with respect to the stock. Therefore, the court dismissed the complaint.
40. *See, e.g., In re Enron Corporation Securities, Derivative & "ERISA" Litigation*, 284 F. Supp. 2d 511 (S.D. Tex. 2003) (discussed below and in Question 34, Example 2).

or otherwise replace the trustee.[41] Moreover, the courts have noted that the language of ERISA expressly imposes upon a directed trustee a duty to determine whether the instructions given to it by the directing named fiduciary are "proper," are "made in accordance with the plan," and are "not contrary to ERISA." While these duties are uncertain in scope, they clearly imply "that the trustee retains certain supervising and investigative duties and that the directed trustee is still bound by the terms of the plan documents and of ERISA and cannot escape its fiduciary or statutory obligations to the plan participants and beneficiaries."[42]

> **Example 1.** Employees of Enron Corporation who were participants in Enron's ESOP, which formed a part of Enron's Section 401(k) plan, brought an action against Enron, officers and directors of Enron, and various plan fiduciaries alleging breaches of fiduciary responsibility under ERISA. Among the many claims brought by the plaintiffs was a claim that the trustee of the Section 401(k) plan, the Northern Trust Company ("Northern"), had breached its fiduciary duties by permitting a lockdown of the Section 401(k) plan and of the ESOP, without adequate notice to participants in the plans, while a new recordkeeper took over responsibility for administration of the plans. During the lockdown period, which ran from October 17, 2001, until November 14, 2001, the price of Enron's stock fell from $33.84 to $10 per share. Northern moved to dismiss the claims against it on the ground that it was acting as a directed trustee and, therefore, had no responsibility with respect to the imposition of the lockdown. Rather, Northern argued that it was simply following the directions of the administrative committees of the two plans, which had discretionary control over the assets of the plans. The court denied the motion to dismiss and ruled that the plaintiffs had stated a claim against Northern, whether it was deemed a directed trustee or not, for proceeding with the lockdown in spite of extraordinary circumstances, including the announcements, shortly before the lockdown, of a $618 million loss in the previous quarter, a $1.2 billion write-down in net worth, and the commencement of an informal investigation of the company by

---

41. *Id.* at 590.
42. *Id.*

the SEC. The court held that that the plaintiffs were entitled to proceed to a trial on the question whether these circumstances should have triggered the trustee's fiduciary duties to the plan participants and beneficiaries to postpone or at least to limit the duration of the scheduled lockdowns, as it had the ability to do.[43]

Issues regarding the scope of the obligations of a directed trustee have arisen in a number of so-called "stock drop" cases. In these cases, trustees have been sued for breach of fiduciary responsibility for failing to sell employer securities at a time when their value was declining rapidly.[44] Many of the trustees involved in these cases were directed trustees who sought to defend themselves by contending that they were following proper directions of named fiduciaries. Difficult questions of interpretation in two basic areas have arisen in determining the scope of a directed trustee's fiduciary obligations in these cases: (1) how is a trustee to determine what is a "proper" direction from a named fiduciary? and (2) what is the nature and extent of a directed trustee's duty to determine whether the directions from the named fiduciary are "in accordance with the terms of the plan" and are "not contrary to ERISA"?

In response to the recent spate of stock-drop cases, the Department of Labor has attempted to provide some much-needed guidance for determining the scope of a directed trustee's fiduciary responsibility in Field Assistance Bulletin No. 2004-03. This bulletin provides guidance particularly on buying, selling, and holding publicly traded employer securities. The Department of Labor stated in the bulletin that in order for a directed trustee to determine whether a direction is in accordance with the plan's terms, the trustee must review all of the plan documents and determine whether the direction is proper. If the terms of the plan document are ambiguous, the Department of Labor takes the position that the trustee should request an interpretation from the named fiduciary for interpreting the plan.

In Field Assistance Bulletin No. 2004-03, the Department of Labor also provided guidance regarding how a directed trustee should deter-

---

43. Id.
44. For a comprehensive discussion of these cases, see Rachal, Shapiro, and Erchberger, "ERISA Fiduciary Duties Regarding 401(k) & ESOP Investments in Employer Stock," ch. 2 in *ERISA Litigation,* 2d ed. (BNA 2005).

mine whether a direction is contrary to ERISA. In this connection, the Department of Labor discussed four situations: (1) prohibited-transaction determinations; (2) prudence determinations; (3) the duty to act on inside (nonpublic) information; and (4) the duty to act on public information. The Department of Labor stated that a directed trustee must follow processes that are designed to avoid prohibited transactions. This obligation can be satisfied by obtaining representations from the named fiduciary that the plan follows procedures for identifying prohibited transactions. Regarding prudence determinations, the Department of Labor stated that a directed trustee does not have an obligation to determine the prudence of every transaction. Rather, the named fiduciary has primary responsibility for this. The Department of Labor went on to state that the directed trustee's obligation to question market transactions involving publicly traded stock on prudence grounds also is quite limited. The primary circumstance in which such an obligation could arise is one in which the directed trustee possesses material nonpublic information regarding a security. In that case, the Department of Labor's view is that, before following a direction that would be affected by the inside information, the directed trustee should inquire about the named fiduciary's knowledge and consideration of the inside information. Finally, the Department of Labor stated in the Bulletin that, absent material nonpublic information, a directed trustee rarely will have an obligation under ERISA to question the prudence of a direction to purchase publicly traded securities at the market price. Mere knowledge of speculative media reports, or even knowledge of an investigation, would not constitute sufficient knowledge giving rise to a duty to act. The Department of Labor noted that stock prices fluctuate as a matter of course and that, therefore, "even a steep drop in a stock's price would not, in and of itself, indicate that a named fiduciary's direction to purchase of hold such stock is imprudent and, therefore, not the proper direction."

> ***Example 2.*** Participants in a Section 401(k) plan sponsored by World-Com, Inc., brought a class action against Merrill Lynch, the trustee of the plan, alleging that Merrill Lynch had breached its fiduciary duty by continuing to purchase WorldCom stock after it learned that the SEC was investigating the company. The court analyzed the plan documents in detail, and it found that Merrill Lynch was subject to

the direction of WorldCom, the named fiduciary. The court held that, as a directed trustee, its fiduciary responsibilities were more limited than those of a discretionary trustee. Relying upon Field Assistance Bulletin No. 2004-03, the court stated that a directed trustee rarely will have an obligation to question the prudence of a direction to purchase publicly traded securities at the market price, unless either (1) the directed trustee possesses material nonpublic information, or (2) the directed trustee knows or should know of "reliable public information that calls into serious question the company's short-term viability as a going concern."[45] The court ruled that Merrill Lynch was entitled to summary judgment because none of the information that it possessed rose to the level of seriousness or certainty that would require it to question the direction it received. For example, the court noted that at the time in question, WorldCom's decline was not out of step with declines suffered by other companies in its industry, and none of the public announcements indicated the impending collapse of the company.[46]

Example 3. Participants in a Section 401(k) plan sponsored by U.S. Airways, Inc., brought a class action against the directed trustee of the company's Section 401(k) plan, alleging that the trustee had breached its fiduciary duty by continuing to hold U.S. Airways stock while the company's fortunes were declining. U.S. Airways declared bankruptcy in August 2002. The court began its analysis by noting that Section 403(a) of ERISA specifically provides that a trustee will have limited authority or discretion when he or she is subject to the directions of another named fiduciary who is not a trustee. The court stated that, by including Section 403(a) in ERISA, Congress plainly meant to create "a subset of ERISA fiduciaries with a statutorily defined duty different from and more narrowly circumscribed than the general duty of ordinary care imposed on other ERISA fiduciaries . . . ."[47] The court went on to state that Congress intended that directed trustees would defer to the investment judgments of the named fiduciary

---

45. *In re WorldCom, Inc. ERISA Litigation*, 354 F. Supp. 2d 423, 449 (S.D.N.Y. 2005).
46. *Id.*
47. *DiFelice v. U.S. Airways, Inc.*, 397 F. Supp. 2d 735, 748 (E.D. Va. 2005).

and not second-guess the wisdom of these judgments. Applying this standard and the guidance provided by the Department of Labor and Field Assistance Bulletin No. 2004-03, the court concluded that a directed trustee has a duty to challenge a direction only after the named fiduciary files for bankruptcy and, even then, only "under circumstances which make it unlikely that there would be any distribution to equity-holders with any value."[48] The plaintiffs' claims against the directed trustee were dismissed.

Q16   Is the plan sponsor a fiduciary?

A plan sponsor is a fiduciary only to the extent that it retains responsibility for or exercises the fiduciary functions described in Question 1. Officers of a company that sponsors an ESOP are fiduciaries when they retain authority for the selection and retention of plan fiduciaries because to that extent they have retained discretionary authority and control regarding the management of the plan.[49] A court has held that a plan sponsor was exercising control over plan assets, and therefore became a fiduciary, when it refused to execute a form that would have permitted the trustees to distribute vested benefits to a terminated employee.[50] However, a plan sponsor is not a fiduciary with respect to the management of plan assets, and the management and administration of the plan, unless it retains authority over these functions on a day-to-day basis.[51]

A plan sponsor does not become a plan fiduciary merely because it establishes, amends, or terminates a plan.[52] These so-called "settlor functions" are not subject to the ERISA fiduciary rules.[53] However, a plan sponsor

---

48. *Id.* at 750.
49. *See Freund v. Marshall & Ilsley Bank*, 485 F. Supp. 629 (W.D. Wis. 1979); DOL Reg. § 2509.75-8, D-4.
50. *Blatt v. Marshall & Lassman*, 812 F.2d 810 (2d Cir. 1987).
51. *Leigh v. Engle*, 727 F.2d 113 (7th Cir. 1984), *remanded*, 669 F. Supp. 1390 (N.D. Ill. 1987), *aff'd*, 858 F.2d 361 (7th Cir. 1988), *cert. denied*, 489 U.S. 1078 (1989) (discussed in Question 27, Example 2).
52. *See Lockheed Corp. v. Spink*, 517 U.S. 882, 890 (1996); *Bennett v. Conrail Matched Savings Plan Admin. Comm.*, 168 F.3d 671, 679 (3d Cir. 1999).
53. DOL letter to Kirk F. Maldonado, dated March 2, 1987, reprinted in *BNA Pension Reporter*, Apr. 6, 1987; *Payonk v. HMW Indus.*, 883 F.2d 221 (3d Cir. 1989).

may be treated as a fiduciary if its representatives make false statements about the plan and if employees reasonably consider these representatives to be acting in the capacity of a plan administrator.[54]

While the decision to amend or terminate an ESOP itself may not be a fiduciary decision, there generally are aspects to a plan termination that are subject to the fiduciary rules of ERISA. For example, if the termination of an ESOP is pursuant to a transaction that requires that voting rights be passed through to the ESOP participants, it is the responsibility of the plan fiduciaries to assure that the participants receive timely and accurate information that is sufficient to enable them to make an informed decision regarding the exercise of their voting rights. See discussion in Questions 59 to 64. In addition, although the authority to determine whether to terminate an employee benefit plan is vested in the plan sponsor's board of directors, the fiduciaries of the plan may have an obligation to assure that the board is acting properly and in compliance with all applicable corporate laws in connection with the termination. See discussion in Question 42.

Q17 Are members of a plan sponsor's board of directors plan fiduciaries?

A person's status as an officer or director of a corporation that maintains an ESOP, in itself, will not make him or her a fiduciary.[55] However, members of the board of directors of an ESOP company will be fiduciaries

---

54. *Varity Corp. v. Howe*, 516 U.S. 489 (1996) (discussed in Question 33).
55. E.g., *Sommers Drug Stores Co. Employee Profit Sharing Trust v. Corrigan Enter. Inc.*, 793 F.2d 1456, 1459–60 (5th Cir. 1986), *cert. denied*, 479 U.S. 1089 (1987); *Leigh v. Engle*, 727 F.2d 113, 135 (7th Cir. 1984), *remanded*, 669 F. Supp. 1390 (N.D. Ill. 1987), *aff'd*, 858 F.2d 361 (7th Cir. 1988), *cert. denied*, 489 U.S. 1078 (1989) (discussed in Question 27, Example 2); *In re WorldCom Inc. ERISA Lit.*, 263 F. Supp. 2d 745, 757-58 (S.D.N.Y. 2003) (discussed in Question 15, Example 2); *Henry v. Champlain Enterprises, Inc.*, 288 F. Supp. 2d 202, 222 (N.D.N.Y. 2003); *Cosgrove v. Circle K Corp.*, 884 F. Supp. 2d 350, 353 (D. Ariz. 1995) (CEO's involvement in transaction on behalf of employer purchasing assets from plan does not make him a fiduciary unless he sought to unduly influence or dominate the trustee's decision); and *Pudela v. Swanson*, 1995 U.S. Dist. LEXIS 2148, 18 (N.D. Ill. 1995) (in absence of allegations that outside directors had authority to vote or otherwise control shares of plan sponsor held by ESOP, outside directors would only be fiduciaries of the ESOP "to the extent

to the extent that they have responsibility for the functions described in Question 1. For example, the board of directors may be responsible for the selection and retention of the plan administrator or of the plan fiduciaries. Then members of the board of directors are fiduciaries for this purpose and must be prudent in the selection of the plan administrators or plan fiduciaries. In addition, the directors also have a duty to monitor the performance of the administrators and fiduciaries that they appoint.[56] The Department of Labor has stated that an appointing fiduciary must follow some type of procedure to periodically review the performance of the appointed fiduciary.[57]

> **Example.** Gary Nutter was the trustee of an ESOP, and he bore responsibility for the investment of plan assets. Nutter also was the corporate secretary and senior vice president of the employer. Gary S. Harris was the president, the CEO, and a shareholder of the employer. Wesley G. Harline was one of several members of the employer's board of directors. The plan documents authorized the board of directors to select the trustee and to appoint successor trustees, and the plan documents directed the establishment of a funding policy and its communication to the trustee. Nutter and Harris caused the plan

---

they exercised discretionary authority or control respecting plan management or administration").

56. See *Keach v. U.S. Trust Co.*, 234 F. Supp. 2d 872, 882–883 (C.D. Ill. 2002), *aff'd*, 419 F.3d 626 (7th Cir. 2005) (although nominally corporate officers had power only to appoint ESOP trustee, they may have exercised "*de facto*" control over transaction because, among other things, they conceived of concept, solicited valuation opinions, set up structure of transaction, and appointed new trustee to implement transaction) (discussed in Question 106, Example 4, and in Question 111); and *Newton v. Van Otterloo*, 756 F. Supp. 1121, 1130–32 (N.D. Ind. 1991) (CEO became a fiduciary by influencing actions of ESOP committee) (discussed in Question 31, Example 2).

57. See DOL Regs. § 2509.7-8, FR-17 Q&A. *Cf. in re Williams Companies ERISA Litigation* 31 EB case 1870, 2003 WL 22794417 at 1, note 1 (N.D. Okla. Oct. 27, 2003) (rejecting Department of Labor's claim in an amicus brief that directors who appointed fiduciaries had a continuous duty to monitor the appointed fiduciaries); and *Newton v. Van Otterloo*, 756 F. Supp. 1121, 1132 (N.D. Ind. 1991) (no breach of duty to monitor appointed fiduciaries absent notice of "possible misadventure" by appointed fiduciaries) (discussed in Question 31, Example 2).

to acquire stock of the employer from themselves and from other directors at prices in excess of fair market value.

The board of directors, including Harline, unanimously approved the appointment of Nutter as trustee. Nutter had no training or experience in managing an employee plan or in investing plan assets. The board never reviewed the performance of the plan investments and did not otherwise monitor Nutter's performance as trustee. Moreover, the board ignored an internal auditor's report and comments of a state regulatory authority indicating irregularities in the investment of plan assets.

The Department of Labor sued Nutter, Harris, and the directors for breach of fiduciary duty. The Department of Labor reached a settlement with all parties except Harline. The court found that Harline was a fiduciary, as a member of the board of directors, and that he was jointly and severally liable for any losses resulting from the breaches of fiduciary duty.[58]

A plan covering employees of a corporation may designate the corporation as the named fiduciary. Then the plan should provide for the designation of specified persons (by name or by title) to carry out specified fiduciary functions under the plan.[59] In the absence of such a designation, the corporation's board of directors (and each individual member) can be treated as a fiduciary, since the board has retained discretionary authority and control with respect to management of the plan.[60] If the responsibility of board members is limited to the selection and retention of fiduciaries, then the liability of board members is limited to that extent.[61]

---

58. *Martin v. Harline*, 15 EBC (BNA) 1138 (D. Utah 1992).
59. ERISA § 405(c)(1)(B); DOL Reg. § 2509.75-5, FR-3.
60. DOL Reg. § 2509.75-8, D-4; *Martin v. Harline*, 15 EBC (BNA) 1138 (D. Utah 1992) (individual member of the board of directors); *Newton v. Van Otterloo*, 756 F. Supp. 1121, 1132 (N.D. Ind. 1991) (power to appoint and remove fiduciaries makes members of company's board of directors fiduciaries) (discussed in Question 31, Example 2).
61. *Batchelor v. Oak Hill Medical Group*, 870 F.2d 1446 (9th Cir. 1989); *Andrade v. Parsons Corp.*, 1990 U.S. Dist. LEXIS 14932, 12 EBC (BNA) 1954 (C.D. Ca. 1990) (discussed in Question 49, Example 3); *Sommers Drugstores Co. Employee*

The members of the plan sponsor's board of directors also may be designated as named fiduciaries. However, if the directors are made named fiduciaries of the plan, their liability may be limited pursuant to a procedure provided for in the plan document for the allocation of fiduciary responsibilities among named fiduciaries or for the designation of persons other than named fiduciaries to carry out fiduciary responsibilities, as discussed in Question 5.

Q18   Can individuals who are officers or employees of a plan sponsor be plan fiduciaries?

Yes. Individuals who are employees of a plan sponsor are plan fiduciaries if they have authority and exercise control regarding the management and administration of the plan or the disposition of plan assets.[62] For example, an individual who has authority and control regarding the appointment of a plan administrator or trustee is a fiduciary for this purpose. This individual must act prudently in making these selections in order to fulfill his or her fiduciary duties.[63] However, officers or employees of a plan sponsor are not fiduciaries if they do not perform fiduciary functions.[64]

Profit Sharing Trust v. Corrigan Enter. Inc. 793 F.2d 1456, *cert. denied*, 479 U.S. 1034 (1987); and *Gelardi v. Pertec Computer Corp.*, 761 F.2d 1323, 1325 (9th Cir. 1985).

62. *Keach v. U.S. Trust Co.*, 234 F. Supp. 2d 872, 882–83 (C.D. Ill. 2002), *aff'd*, 419 F.3d 626 (7th Cir. 2005) (CEO was a fiduciary because he exercised "*de facto*" control by conceiving concept for ESOP transaction, soliciting valuation opinions, structuring transaction, and appointing new trustee to review and implement transaction) (discussed in Question 106, Example 4, and in Question 111).

63. *Martin v. Harline*, 15 EBC 1138 (D. Utah 1992) (discussed in Question 17); *see also Newton v. Van Otterloo*, 756 F. Supp. 1121 (N.D. Ind. 1991) (president of ESOP company held to be a fiduciary by directing ESOP administrative committee with respect to solicitation of voting instructions in board of directors election) (discussed in Question 31, Example 2).

64. For example, in *Lower v. Albert*, 187 F.3d 636 (6th Cir. 1999), members of a management group that also were serving as the administrators of an ESOP were held not to be acting in a fiduciary capacity when they acquired a controlling interest in the ESOP company. The plaintiff alleged that the managers violated their fiduciary duties as administrators of the ESOP by not offering

Q19 Can corporate officers and directors be plan fiduciaries for some purposes, but not for others?

Yes.[65] ERISA states that "a person is a fiduciary with respect to a plan *to the extent* (1) he exercises any discretionary authority or discretionary control respecting management of such plan or exercises any authority or control respecting management or disposition of its assets . . . ."[66] An individual may serve both as a fiduciary and as an officer or other representative of a plan sponsor, and that individual then will serve dual roles with different duties and responsibilities.[67] Plan administrators who also are officers of the plan sponsor assume fiduciary status only when and to the extent that they act as plan administrators, and not when they conduct business unregulated by ERISA.[68] Therefore, when a person who is both an ERISA fiduciary and a corporate officer undertakes day-to-day business operations that may have a collateral effect on employee benefits, ERISA does not require that he or she operate solely in the interest of plan participants.[69]

---

the stock to the plan. The court held that in deciding to purchase the company stock for their own benefit, the members of the management group were not managing or administering the ESOP or its assets. *See also Berlin v. Michigan Bell Telephone Co.*, 858 F.2d 1154, 1161 n. 5 (6th Cir. 1988).

65. *See Plumb v. Fluid Pump Service, Inc.*, 124 F. 3d 849, 854 (7th Cir. 1997).
66. ERISA, § 3(21)(A) (emphasis added).
67. ERISA, § 408(c)(3).
68. *Canale v. Yegen*, 782 F. Supp. 963, 967 (D. N.J. 1992) (quoting *Payonk v. HM Industries, Inc.*, 883 F. 2d 221, 227 [3d Cir. 1989]). *See also Martin v. Feilen*, 965 F. 2d 660, 666 (8th Cir. 1992), *cert. denied*, 113 S. Ct. 979 (1993) (rejecting argument by Secretary of Labor for a broad application of ERISA fiduciary duty, stating that even though "[v]irtually all of an employer's significant business decisions affect the *value* of its stock, and therefore the benefits that ESOP plan participants will ultimately receive," ERISA fiduciary duties attach only when an individual invests the ESOP's assets or administers the plan) (discussed in Question 27, Example 1).
69. *Hickman v. Tosco Corp.*, 840 F. 2d 564, 566 (8th Cir. 1988) ("ERISA does not prohibit an employer from acting in accordance with its interest as an employer when not administering the plan or investing its assets") (quoting *Phillips v. Amoco Oil Co.*, 614 F. Supp. 694, 718 (N.D. Ala. 1985), *aff'd*, 799 F. 2d 1464, 1471 [11th Cir. 1986]); and *Armstrong v. Amsted Industries, Inc.*, 2004 WL 1745774

In determining whether a person who serves both as a corporate officer or director and as an ESOP fiduciary is subject to the ERISA fiduciary rules with respect to any particular act or omission, it must be determined whether the act or omission relates to a matter or transaction that involves plan assets. The duties imposed upon fiduciaries of employee benefit plans by ERISA apply only to transactions that involve the assets of the plan and to activities that involve the administration of the plan.[70] In the case of an ESOP, the plan assets are the shares of the plan sponsor (and any other assets held by the plan). The Department of Labor's regulations interpreting ERISA make clear that properties acquired and owned by the plan sponsor are *not* themselves plan assets. Where an employee benefit plan, such as an ESOP, invests in an operating company, the plan's assets include its investment, but do not include any of the underlying assets of the operating company.[71]

Q20 What is the plan administrator?

The plan administrator manages the day-to-day affairs of the plan. Among the responsibilities of the plan administrator are the hiring of attorneys, accountants, actuaries, and other plan professionals, determining plan eligibility and other rights of participants, ruling on benefit claims, preparing reports to be filed with governmental agencies, preparing reports for participants, and maintaining plan records.

The plan administrator is generally specifically designated by the plan document as the plan administrator. The document may designate a plan administrator:

(N.D. Ill.), *rev'd on other grounds*, 446 F.3d 728 (7th Cir. 2006) (discussed in Question 29, Example 1, and in Question 43).

70. *Martin v. Feilen*, 965 F. 2d 660, 666 (8th Cir. 1992), *cert. denied*, 113 S. Ct. 979 (1993) (discussed in Question 27, Example 1).

71. DOL Regs. § 2510.3-101(a)(2). *See Armstrong v. Amsted Industries, Inc.*, 2004 WL 1745774 (N.D. Ill.), *rev'd on other grounds*, 446 F.3d 728 (7th Cir. 2006) (claims against officers of an ESOP company who also were fiduciaries, relating to the acquisition of another corporation, dismissed on ground that decision to acquire the other corporation was a business decision that did not trigger a fiduciary duty under ERISA) (discussed in Question 29, Example 1, and in Question 43).

- by name,
- by reference to the person or group holding a named position,
- by reference to a procedure for designating an administrator, or
- by reference to the person or group charged with the specific responsibilities of plan administrator.

A plan may provide for the allocation of specific responsibilities of plan administration among named persons and for named persons to designate others to carry out particular responsibilities.

Q21   Are plan administrators ESOP fiduciaries?

Generally a plan administrator is a fiduciary under ERISA because the administrator has discretionary authority with respect to the administration of the plan.[72] For example, in one case, a court found that a plan administration committee was a named fiduciary of an ESOP because it was responsible for maintenance of the participants' ESOP accounts, automatic enrollment of employees, and valuation of the trust fund. Additionally, the committee had authority to establish investment guidelines and to determine requirements and objectives of the plan relating to the investment of the trust fund. The court determined, however, that the committee was a fiduciary only with respect to its own functions. It was not a fiduciary with respect to investment assets over which it had no discretionary authority or control.[73]

Q22   When are professional service providers considered plan fiduciaries?

A professional service provider can become a fiduciary of a plan if he or she has or exercises discretionary authority, control, or responsibility with

---

72. ERISA § 3(21)(A); *Moench v. Robertson*, 62 F.3d 553 (3d Cir. 1995) (ESOP committee members held to be fiduciaries because they had authority to direct the investment of plan assets) (discussed in Question 55, Example 1).
73. *Moench v. Robertson*, 62 F.3d 553 (3d Cir. 1995) (discussed in Question 55, Example 1).

respect to the plan, its assets, or its administration, even if these activities are not authorized by the named fiduciaries or by other fiduciaries.[74]

Example. Accountants were held to be fiduciaries in a case where they effectively exercised control over the assets of an ESOP in complex commercial transactions and engaged in acts of self-dealing. The accountants recommended transactions, structured deals, and provided investment advice. None of the other corporate officers possessed the expertise in accounting and employee benefits law needed to arrange the transactions, and the accountants were corporate insiders and used their positions of trust and confidence to involve the ESOP in transactions in which they had a personal interest.[75]

A professional service provider is not considered a plan fiduciary solely by reason of rendering professional services. Most recent cases have held that professional service providers acting in their usual professional functions do not thereby possess or exercise the necessary discretionary authority, control, or responsibility in connection with the employee benefit plan to cause them to be fiduciaries under ERISA.[76] When professional service providers are not fiduciaries, they generally will not have fiduciary liability for compensatory money damages, even if they are knowing participants in a fiduciary breach.[77] However, if they

---

74. ERISA § 3(21)(A); DOL Reg. § 2509.75-5, D-1; *Olson v. E. F. Hutton & Co.*, 957 F.2d 622 (8th Cir. 1992) (broker).
75. *Martin v. Feilen*, 965 F.2d 660 (8th Cir. 1992), *cert. denied*, 113 S.Ct. 979 (1993) (this case is discussed in more detail in Question 27, Example 1).
76. *Mertens v. Hewitt Assocs.*, 508 U.S. 248 (1993) (actuaries); *Useden v. Acker*, 947 F.2d 1563, 1577–78 (11th Cir. 1991) (law firm and bank); *Pappas v. Buck Consultants, Inc*, 923 F.2d 531 (7th Cir. 1991) (actuaries); *Anoka Orthopaedic Assocs., PA v. Lechner*, 910 F.2d 514 (8th Cir. 1990) (attorneys and consultants); *Painters of Philadelphia Dist. Council No. 21 Welfare Fund v. Price Waterhouse*, 879 F.2d 1146 (3d Cir. 1989) (accountants); *Nieto v. Ecker*, 845 F.2d 868 (9th Cir. 1988) (attorney); *Yeseta v. Baima*, 837 F.2d 380 (9th Cir. 1988) (attorney and accountant); *Keach v. U.S. Trust Co.*, 2002 WL 31846239 (C.D. Ill.) (ESOP trustee's financial advisor); and *Keach v. U.S. Trust Co.*, 313 F. Supp. 2d 818 (C.D. Ill. 2004) (financial advisor to plan sponsor) (other aspects of this case are discussed in Question 106, Example 4).
77. *Mertens v. Hewitt Assocs.*, 508 U.S. 248 (1993).

knowingly participate in a "prohibited transaction," they may be liable for excise taxes and penalties and they may be required to take corrective actions to undo the prohibited transaction.[78] (See the discussion of prohibited transactions in Questions 70–91.)

Q23 If a professional service provider who is a member of a professional firm renders services to a plan in a fiduciary capacity, can the other members of the professional firm be considered fiduciaries?

The other members of the professional firm can be considered fiduciaries, depending on the circumstances. If the other members directly or indirectly have or exercise discretionary authority, control, or responsibility with respect to the plan, its assets, or its administration, the other members will be considered fiduciaries.[79]

> *Planning Pointer.* It is not uncommon for the corporate secretary of a plan sponsor to be an attorney. Moreover, the attorney's law firm commonly serves as counsel to the employer and the employee benefit plans sponsored by the employer. These roles do not automatically make the law firm a fiduciary. However, if the corporate secretary-attorney also serves as trustee or named fiduciary, then in order to limit the possibility that the law firm would be treated as a fiduciary, the corporate secretary-attorney should avoid taking an active role in rendering legal advice with respect to the plan.

Q24 When can an in-house professional service provider be considered a plan fiduciary?

To the extent that the in-house professional service provider possesses or exercises any of the fiduciary functions described in Question 1, he or she will be considered a plan fiduciary. The offices and positions of an in-house professional service provider could include the functions of

---

78. Code § 4975(a) and (b) (excise taxes on prohibited transactions); ERISA § 502(i) (penalty for prohibited transaction).
79. *See Useden v. Acker*, 947 F.2d 1563, 1577-78 (11th Cir. 1991) (law firm not fiduciary).

plan administrator or trustee, which are generally fiduciary functions. Other offices and positions should be examined to determine whether they involve the performance of any of the fiduciary functions described above. The title of the designation is not determinative. (See the discussion of offices and positions that can result in fiduciary status in Question 4.) In-house professional service providers (such as in-house counsel) who effectively have the final authority to approve benefit payments in cases where a dispute exists as to the interpretation of plan provisions relating to eligibility for plan benefits are fiduciaries within the meaning of ERISA.[80]

Q25 May other plan fiduciaries serve as professional service providers?

Generally, yes. Any person may serve a plan in both a fiduciary and non-fiduciary capacity or in more than one fiduciary capacity.[81] However, the accountant retained by an employee benefit plan for purposes of auditing and rendering an opinion on the financial information that may be required to be included in the annual report (Form 5500) filed with the Department of Labor must in fact be independent of the plan for which the accountant renders an opinion.[82]

---

80. DOL Reg. § 2509.75-8, D-3.
81. ERISA § 402(c)(1).
82. ERISA § 103(a)(3)(A); DOL Reg. § 2509.75-9.

CHAPTER 2

FIDUCIARY DUTIES

Contents

General **31**
Q26   What are the primary fiduciary duties under ERISA? 31

The Exclusive Benefit Rule **32**
Q27   What is required for a fiduciary to satisfy the "exclusive benefit" requirement? 32
Q28   Is it a violation of the exclusive benefit requirement if the fiduciary's action also benefits the employer? 34
Q29   If officers or directors of the plan sponsor also serve as plan fiduciaries, can they be held liable for business decisions that adversely affect the value of stock held by the ESOP? 35
Q30   May ESOP fiduciaries take into account whether a proposed transaction will preserve employment for plan participants? 36
Q31   May ESOP trustees vote themselves on to the plan sponsor's board of directors? 37
Q32   Does ERISA prohibit a bank from serving simultaneously as an ESOP trustee and as a lender to the plan sponsor? 39
Q33   Can an ESOP fiduciary be held liable for misrepresenting facts regarding the plan or the plan sponsor? 40
Q34   Can an ESOP fiduciary be held liable for withholding material information regarding the plan sponsor? 41
Q35   Does an employer have a duty to disclose information about proposed changes to an ESOP? 44
Q36   Must an ESOP fiduciary turn over a copy of the valuation report to a participant who requests to see it? 44

The Prudence Standard **45**
Q37   What must a fiduciary do to satisfy the prudence requirement? 45
Q38   What is the legal standard for determining whether a fiduciary's acts are prudent? 45

29

Q39	Are a fiduciary's actions judged by the standard of an ordinary person or that of an expert? 46
Q40	What other standards do courts employ in determining whether an ESOP fiduciary has satisfied the prudence requirement? 46
Q41	How does the prudence requirement apply with respect to voting stock of the sponsoring employer? 47
Q42	Should an ESOP fiduciary monitor or seek to influence the management of the plan sponsor? 47
Q43	How does the prudence requirement apply with respect to forecasting an ESOP company's repurchase obligation? 49
Q44	What role should an ESOP fiduciary play in determining the appropriateness of executive compensation? 51
Q45	Can an ESOP fiduciary avoid liability for an imprudent decision by establishing that he or she acted in good faith? 53
Q46	What is the standard of review applied by courts in evaluating the prudence of the conduct of an independent ESOP fiduciary? 53
Q47	What is the standard of review applied by courts in evaluating the prudence of the conduct of an ESOP fiduciary who has a conflict of interest? 54
Q48	What is the difference between "substantive prudence" and "procedural prudence"? 55
Q49	What constitutes procedural prudence? 56
Q50	Does an ESOP fiduciary have an obligation to seek the assistance of an expert to satisfy the prudence requirement? 60
Q51	Will an ESOP fiduciary be absolved of liability if he or she acts in reliance upon the advice of a qualified independent adviser? 60
Q52	Can a trustee be held liable for an imprudent resignation? 61

Diversification **63**

Q53	What is required for a fiduciary to satisfy the ERISA diversification requirement? 63
Q54	If an ESOP holds assets in addition to employer stock, do the diversification rules apply? 63
Q55	Are there any other circumstances under which an ESOP fiduciary has a duty to diversify plan assets? 64
Q56	What are the primary factors for prudent diversification? 69

Following Plan Documents..69

Q57 What is required for a fiduciary to discharge his or her responsibilities in accordance with plan documents? 69

Q58 What is pass-through voting? 70

Q59 If the plan document provides for pass-through voting, is the ESOP trustee obligated to follow voting directions that he or she receives from plan participants and beneficiaries? 70

Q60 Can there be circumstances under which an ESOP fiduciary must disregard voting directions from plan participants and beneficiaries even though the plan document provides for pass-through voting? 71

Q61 What procedures should an ESOP trustee follow in soliciting voting instructions? 72

Q62 What specific actions should an ESOP trustee take to ensure that pass-through voting is conducted on a free and fair basis? 72

Q63 What is "mirror voting"? 73

Q64 Are ESOP trustees required to comply with mirror-voting provisions? 73

Q65 May an ESOP plan document grant to plan participants the authority to direct the trustee with regard to tendering of stock allocated to their accounts in response to a tender offer? 74

Q66 If the plan document provides that any offer to purchase shares of the plan sponsor must be passed through to the participants, must the ESOP trustee always follow the participants' directions? 75

Q67 What action should an ESOP trustee take to ensure that participants' directions regarding response to a tender offer are proper? 76

Q68 What is "mirror tendering"? 76

Q69 Are mirror-tendering provisions in ESOP plan documents valid? 77

General

Q26 What are the primary fiduciary duties under ERISA?

The primary duties of a fiduciary under ERISA are the following:

1. to act for the exclusive benefit of plan participants and beneficiaries;

2. to act prudently;
3. to diversify the investment of the plan assets; and
4. to act in accordance with plan documents.[83]

In the case of an ESOP (or other "eligible individual account plan"), the diversification requirement and the prudence requirement (to the extent it requires diversification) are not violated by the acquisition or holding of qualifying employer securities.[84] See Question 80 for a discussion of what constitutes "qualifying employer securities."

The Exclusive Benefit Rule

Q27 What is required for a fiduciary to satisfy the "exclusive benefit" requirement?

To satisfy the exclusive benefit requirement, a fiduciary must act solely in the interest of the plan's participants and beneficiaries and for the exclusive purpose of providing benefits to participants and their beneficiaries and defraying reasonable administrative expenses of the plan.[85] As one court has formulated this rule, a fiduciary's decisions must be made "with an eye single to the interests of the participants and beneficiaries."[86] Another court has developed the following three-pronged test for determining whether a plan fiduciary has violated the exclusive benefit requirement:

1. First, the court must ask whether the conflict of interest is so great that it is virtually impossible for the fiduciary to discharge his or her duties with an eye single to the interests of the participants and beneficiaries.

2. If not, then the court must determine whether the fiduciary engaged in an intensive and independent investigation of options to ensure that the action taken was in the participants' best interests.

---

83. ERISA § 404(a)(1).
84. ERISA § 404(a)(2).
85. ERISA § 404(a)(1)(A).
86. *Donovan v. Bierwirth*, 680 F.2d 263, 271 (2d Cir. 1982), *cert. denied*, 459 U.S. 1069 (1982) (discussed in Question 49, Example 1, and Question 122).

3. Then the court must determine the extent to which the use of the plan assets tracked the best interests of another party.[87]

Example 1. The controlling shareholders and directors of a corporation, together with the corporation's accountants, engaged in self-dealing using the assets of the corporation's ESOP. These individuals also were fiduciaries of the ESOP by reason of their control over plan assets. Among other things, they caused the corporation to assume a high-interest loan obligation of a company partially owned by the accountants in exchange for inadequate consideration, and they caused the ESOP to buy and sell shares of the sponsoring employer's stock at prices less favorable to the ESOP than to others. The Department of Labor brought an action against the fiduciaries, seeking money damages and an order enjoining them from providing future services to other employee benefit plans. In evaluating the conduct of the fiduciaries, the court noted that, while self-dealing and conflicts of interest are not inherently unlawful, ESOP fiduciaries with dual loyalties must make a careful and impartial investigation of alternatives and normally should obtain impartial guidance from disinterested outside advisors. The fiduciaries were held to have violated the exclusive benefit rule, as well as the duty of prudence.[88]

Example 2. The trustees of a profit sharing trust invested approximately 30% of the trust's assets in three companies for the purpose of assisting various parties related to the trustees either to obtain control of the companies or to earn substantial "control premiums." The court ruled that the trustees failed to act solely in the interests of the plan participants because they were actively engaged in the contests for control of the companies in which they invested the trust's funds, because they failed to make an intensive independent investigation of the investment options available to the trust, and

---

87. *Leigh v. Engle*, 727 F.2d 113, 125–26 (7th Cir. 1984), *remanded*, 669 F. Supp. 1390 (N.D. Ill. 1987), *aff'd*, 858 F.2d 361 (7th Cir. 1988), *cert. denied*, 489 U.S. 1078 (1989). *Accord, Newton v. Van Otterloo*, 756 F. Supp. 1121 (N.D. Ind. 1991) (discussed in Question 30, Example 2).
88. *Martin v. Feilen*, 965 F.2d 660 (8th Cir. 1992), *cert. denied*, 113 S. Ct. 979 (1993).

because their decisions regarding the investment of the trust's funds never deviated from the best interests of the parties seeking control of the companies in which the trust funds were invested and with whom the trustees had a relationship.[89]

Example 3. The trustees of an ESOP were officers and directors of the plan sponsor. The plan provided that each participant would instruct the trustees how to vote the shares of company stock allocated to his or her account. During a proxy contest, the trustees solicited voting directions from the plan participants on behalf of management. The trustees included misleading and biased information in the proxy solicitation, and they refused to include materials prepared by the opposition. In addition, the trustees voted the unallocated shares in their own favor without evaluating whether voting for the opposition would have been in the best interests of the participants. The court held that it was improper for the trustees to advise the participants regarding how to vote, and it ordered the removal of the management trustees and the appointment of a neutral trustee in their place.[90]

Q28 Is it a violation of the exclusive benefit requirement if the fiduciary's action also benefits the employer?

A transaction may incidentally benefit the employer without resulting in a violation of the exclusive benefit rule if, after a careful, thorough, and impartial inquiry, the fiduciary reasonably concludes that the transaction is in the interest of plan participants and beneficiaries.[91]

Planning Pointer. Where a fiduciary sees the possibility of a conflict of interest between the plan participants and beneficiaries on the one hand, and another party to a transaction (such as the sponsoring employer) on the other hand, the fiduciary should promptly seek

---

89. *Leigh v. Engle*, 727 F.2d 113 (7th Cir. 1984), *remanded*, 669 F. Supp. 1390 (N.D. Ill. 1987), *aff'd*, 858 F.2d 361 (7th Cir. 1988), *cert. denied*, 489 U.S. 1078 (1989) (also discussed in Question 123).
90. *Shoen v. AMERCO*, 885 F. Supp. 1332 (D. Nev. 1994).
91. *Donovan v. Bierwirth*, 680 F.2d 263, 271 (2d Cir 1982), *cert. denied*, 459 U.S. 1069 (1982) (discussed in Question 49, Example 1, and in Question 122).

the advice of a competent, independent advisor. It may be necessary under these kinds of circumstances for the fiduciary to withdraw from participating in any decision that would potentially present a conflict of interest or to resign as a fiduciary before being called upon to participate in the decision.[92]

Q29 If officers or directors of the plan sponsor also serve as plan fiduciaries, can they be held liable for business decisions that adversely affect the value of stock held by the ESOP?

The business decisions made by an employer that sponsors an ESOP often will indirectly affect the value of its stock and, therefore, the value of the benefits to be received by ESOP participants. If the persons who make the corporate decisions also are ESOP fiduciaries, they will not be subject to liability for breach of ERISA fiduciary duties with respect to decisions that are made in their capacities as corporate officers and not in their capacities as plan administrators or fiduciaries. The fiduciary duties imposed by ERISA apply only to transactions that involve investing the assets of the ESOP.[93]

> ***Example 1.*** Employees of Amsted Industries, Inc., brought a class action against the company, various officers of the company, members of the company's ESOP committee, and the trustee of the company's ESOP alleging that the defendants had violated their fiduciary duties by, among other things, approving a large corporate acquisition. Shortly after the acquisition, the value of Amsted's stock declined sharply. The court dismissed this claim on the ground that the acquisition did not involve authority or control over assets of the ESOP. Although the members of the ESOP committee and other individual defendants were fiduciaries with respect to the ESOP, the court stated that they needed to don their "fiduciary hat" only when exercising authority or control over ESOP assets or administering the plan. The court went on to state that although the assets of the

---

92. DOL Adv. Op. Ltr. No. 84-09A, n. 2 (Feb. 16, 1984); DOL Adv. Op. Ltr. No. 79-42A (July 5, 1979); DOL Reg. § 2550.408b-2(e)(2) and 2(f) (ex. 7).
93. See discussion in Question 19.

Amsted ESOP were the shares of Amsted, properties acquired and owned by Amsted were not plan assets. Therefore, the court ruled that the challenged acquisition did not involve authority or control over plan assets.[94]

Example 2. Company executives, who also were fiduciaries of the company's pension plan, refused to allow certain employees to remain on the payroll after a plant was sold so that they could become eligible for early retirement benefits. The terminated employees sued the company executives and claimed that they had a duty, as plan fiduciaries, to act in the manner most beneficial to the plan participants. The court held that the company executives were not subject to the ERISA fiduciary rules because their action was a "day-to-day corporate business transaction" made in their capacity as corporate officers, not as plan administrators.[95]

Although corporate officers who also serve as ESOP fiduciaries cannot be held liable under ERISA for corporate transactions that do not involve managing plan assets or administering the plan, they may have a duty to challenge transactions that constitute a breach of corporate law duties to stockholders, including the ESOP.[96]

Q30 May ESOP fiduciaries take into account whether a proposed transaction will preserve employment for plan participants?

Both the Department of Labor and the Internal Revenue Service (IRS) take the position that ESOP fiduciaries must consider the interests of plan participants solely in their capacities as participants in a plan providing for retirement benefits. Under this view, the fiduciaries must not take into consideration whether a given decision will preserve employment

---

94. *Armstrong v. Amsted Industries, Inc.*, 2004 WL 1745774 (N.D. Ill.), *rev'd on other grounds*, 446 F.3d 728 (7th Cir. 2006) (also discussed in Question 43).
95. *Hickman v. Tosco Corp.*, 840 F.2d 564, at 566-67 (8th Cir. 1988). *But see Martin v. Feilen*, 965 F.2d 660, 665–66 (8th Cir. 1992), *cert. denied*, 113 S. Ct. 979 (1993) (discussed in Question 27, Example 1).
96. *See Martin v. Feilen*, 965 F.2d 660, ____ (8th Cir. 1992), *cert. denied*, 113 S. Ct. 979 (1993) (discussed in Question 27, Example 1).

for plan participants. Rather, the fiduciaries must consider exclusively the financial interests of the participants in their future retirement income.[97] However, one federal court has held that fiduciaries acted properly when using a minority-interest discount for the valuation of stock distributed to participants, despite the fact that the plan owned a majority of the plan sponsor's stock, in furtherance of the plan's goal of maintaining continued employee ownership of the plan sponsor.[98]

Q31 May ESOP trustees vote themselves on to the plan sponsor's board of directors?

ESOP trustees who are not subject to direction as to the voting of the employer securities that they hold may vote for themselves in board of director elections. If the ESOP trustees hold a controlling interest in the plan sponsor, they will have the power to secure for themselves control of the plan sponsor. Since the trustees are selected by the board of directors of the plan sponsor, where the directors also serve as the ESOP trustees the result may be "management entrenchment." In itself, this does not constitute a violation of ERISA.[99] However, where there is entrenched management in an ESOP company, and where the ESOP trustees have conflicts of interest, allegations of improper conduct by the ESOP trustees will be given the benefit of the doubt.[100]

> *Example 1.* In 1996, employees of North American Rayon Corporation ("NAR") brought an action against the trustee of NAR's ESOP, members of the ESOP administrative committee, and members of NAR's board of directors. The ESOP was administered by the committee, members of which were appointed by the board of directors. The committee directed the trustee as to the voting of the NAR shares held by the ESOP in board of director elections. The plaintiffs complained that the defendants who served both on the committee and the board violated their fiduciary duties by directing the trustee to

---

97. GCM 39870, April 7, 1992.
98. *Foltz v. U.S. News & World Report*, 865 F.2d 364 (D.C. Cir. 1989).
99. *Grindstaff v. Green*, 21 EBC (BNA) 2249 (6th Cir. 1998).
100. *See, e.g., Newton v. Van Otterloo*, 756 F. Supp. 1121 (N.D. Ind. 1991); and *O'Neill v. Davis*, 721 F. Supp. 1013 (N.D. Ill. 1989).

vote for the defendants in the regular annual election of the board and then, in turn, once elected to the board, by appointing themselves to the committee. The court characterized the plaintiffs' complaint as an allegation that "management entrenchment" was a violation of ERISA. The court held that this was not sufficient to state a claim. The court stated that the mere voting of an ESOP's stock by incumbent directors to perpetuate their positions, by itself, did not constitute a breach of fiduciary duty.[101]

Example 2. In 1989, an ESOP sponsored by South Bend Lathe, Inc. ("SBL"), held 81% of SBL's outstanding stock. Most of the remaining SBL stock was held by its president, John Van Otterloo. The ESOP plan document provided that the trustee would vote the SBL stock that it held in accordance with instructions from the ESOP committee. The committee was required to solicit voting instructions from participants whose shares were vested, but the committee had discretion to determine how to instruct the trustee to vote shares which were not vested and how to vote vested shares as to which the committee did not receive instruction from the participants. At the 1989 shareholders' meeting, the committee directed the trustee to abstain from voting unallocated shares and shares with respect to which the committee had not received instructions from the participants. As a result, 15,500 of the shares held by the ESOP were not voted. Of the remaining 7,000 shares held by the ESOP, the trustee cast 5,100 shares against the management slate and 1,900 for the management slate. On the strength of Mr. Van Otterloo's vote of his own 5,000 shares, he was reelected to the SBL board of directors, along with his other nominees, and SBL's articles of incorporation were amended to provide staggered three-year terms for directors.

Two of the members of the committee, who were outvoted, brought an action against the remaining committee members, Mr. Van Otterloo, the members of SBL's board of directors, and the trustee, alleging breach of fiduciary duty in connection with the 1989 shareholder vote. The court granted summary judgment in favor of the plaintiffs and against the other members of the committee and against Mr. Van Otterloo. With respect to the committee members,

---

101. *Grindstaff v. Green*, 21 EBC (BNA) 2249 (6th Cir. 1998).

the court noted that they were members of SBL management and, therefore, had divided loyalties. This required them to engage in a careful investigation of their options with respect to how to vote the SBL shares, which the court found that the committee members had failed to do. With respect to Mr. Van Otterloo, the court found that he was a fiduciary, because he had exercised authority and control over the committee, and that he also failed to carefully investigate the options available to the committee with respect to the voting of the shares. Members of the board of directors of SBL were absolved of liability because the court found that they had not been made aware of any improper actions by the committee members. The court also absolved the trustee of liability because nothing in the record would charge the trustee with knowledge of the failure by the committee members to engage in a careful investigation before directing the trustee as to how to vote the shares.[102]

Q32 Does ERISA prohibit a bank from serving simultaneously as an ESOP trustee and as a lender to the plan sponsor?

The Department of Labor has interpreted the requirement that fiduciaries of an employee benefit plan must act "solely in the interest" of the plan participants and of their beneficiaries to prohibit a bank that has loans outstanding with a particular company from serving as the trustee of that company's ESOP.[103] A federal court of appeals has held that a bank was not prohibited from serving as the trustee of an ESOP when it had loaned funds to the plan sponsor, but in that case the ESOP plan document expressly provided that the plan sponsor would direct the trustee with respect to all investment decisions.[104]

In another case, a court held that a bank had not violated ERISA when it became the trustee of a plan that held shares of a company to which

---

102. *Newton v. Van Otterloo*, 756 F. Supp. 1121 (N.D. Ind. 1991).
103. DOL Adv. Op. Ltr. No. 76-32 (Jan 13, 1976). See also ERISA § 406(b)(2), which prohibits a plan fiduciary from acting in any transaction involving the plan on behalf of a party whose interests are adverse to the interests of the plan or to the interests of the plan participants or their beneficiaries.
104 *Ershick v. United Missouri Bank of Kansas City*, 948 F.2d 660 (10th Cir. 1991) (discussed in Question 46).

the bank had made a loan. The bank later refused to extend the term of its loan, and the borrowing company subsequently declared bankruptcy with only enough assets to repay the bank loan. The participants in the plan that had invested in the borrower brought an action against the bank, but the court held for the bank on the grounds that it was not prohibited from holding positions of dual loyalties and because the plaintiffs could not establish a causal connection between the alleged breach of fiduciary responsibility and the loss incurred by their plan.[105]

Q33 Can an ESOP fiduciary be held liable for misrepresenting facts regarding the plan or the plan sponsor?

Yes. An ESOP fiduciary violates his or her obligation to act for the exclusive benefit of plan participants if he or she makes material misrepresentations regarding the plan, whether negligently or intentionally.[106] However, an ERISA fiduciary has no "duty of clairvoyance," and a fiduciary is not under any obligation "to offer precise predictions about future changes to its plan."[107] Moreover, a truthful statement, made by a fiduciary in good faith, will not give rise to liability simply because participants misunderstood the statement.[108]

---

105. *Friend v. Sanwa Bank California*, 35 F.3d 466 (9th Cir. 1994).
106. *Anderson v. Resolution Trust Corp.*, 66 F.3d 956 (8th Cir. 1995) (claim against fiduciaries remanded to trial court for determination whether fiduciaries led employees to believe that benefits still were accruing by stating, at information meetings and in written bulletins, that all benefits were intact or unchanged when, in fact, pension benefits had been suspended); *Barker v. American Mobile Power Corp.*, 64 F.3d 1397 (9th Cir. 1995) (plan fiduciary held liable for breach of duty for failing to investigate the mishandling of plan funds and for later misleading participants as to the availability of their retirement benefits); and *Berlin v. Michigan Bell Tel. Co.*, 858 F.2d 1154, 1163–64 (6th Cir. 1988) (claim against fiduciaries remanded to trial court for determination whether fiduciaries misled potential participants in a severance-pay plan regarding likelihood of implementation of plan after serious consideration of plan offering commenced).
107. *Fischer v. Philadelphia Electric Co.*, 994 F.2d 130, 135 (3d Cir. 1993).
108. *Barnes v. Lacy*, 927 F.2d 539, 544 (11th Cir. 1991).

Example. In the mid-1980s, Varity Corporation created Massey Combines for the purpose of receiving a transfer of employees of Varity's subsidiary, Massey-Ferguson, Inc., together with benefit plans and other debts of Massey-Ferguson, which was losing money. Varity called a special meeting of the employees of Massey-Ferguson and promised that their benefits would remain secure if they transferred to Massey Combines. After the meeting, approximately 1,500 employees agreed to the transfer. Within a couple of years, Massey Combines went into receivership and the employees lost their benefits. The employees brought an action against Varity for breach of fiduciary duty. Varity argued that it was not acting as a fiduciary, but solely as an employer, when it urged the employees of Massey-Ferguson to transfer to Massey Combines. The Supreme Court concluded otherwise and found that when Varity called the meeting to represent that the transfer would not threaten the benefits to which the employees were entitled, it was acting in its fiduciary capacity as a plan administrator. The Court found that Varity expected Massey Combines to fail and ruled that Varity had breached its duty of loyalty by deceiving the plan participants in order to save itself money at the participants' expense.[109]

Q34 Can an ESOP fiduciary be held liable for withholding material information regarding the plan sponsor?

Where plan participants have decision-making authority with respect to their investments, such as in Section 401(k) plans where employer stock is an investment alternative, fiduciaries may have an affirmative duty to warn plan participants of material adverse information about their investments in employer securities. However, this duty may conflict with the disclosure obligations imposed under the federal securities laws in connection with purchases and sales of securities. The courts have not been consistent in their efforts to resolve this conflict.

Example 1. Participants in a combined Section 401(k) plan and ESOP sponsored by McKesson HBOC, Inc., brought a claim against fiduciaries of the plan alleging that the fiduciaries had violated ERISA

---

109. *Varity Corp. v. Howe*, 516 U.S. 489 (1996).

by failing to sell employer securities after they became aware of financial irregularities involving the plan sponsor. The court found that the fiduciaries could not have sold the employer securities and not disclosed the financial improprieties without violating the federal securities laws. It held that the fiduciaries were not obligated to violate the securities laws to protect the interests of the plan participants. Although the fiduciaries could have disclosed the information publicly before selling the stock, that would have swiftly resulted in a market adjustment that would have prevented the fiduciaries from selling the stock at a price higher than the price to which it declined after disclosure subsequently was made. Therefore, the court dismissed the claim because there could be no damages flowing from the alleged breach.[110]

Example 2. In the highly publicized Enron litigation, employees of Enron Corporation who participated in three employee pension benefit plans sponsored by Enron, including an ESOP, alleged that members of the ESOP administrative committee and members of the compensation committee of Enron's board of directors breached their duties of loyalty to the plan participants by misleading the participants about Enron's financial condition and performance and about its accounting manipulations while, at the same time, inducing the

---

110. *In re: McKesson HBOC, Inc. ERISA Lit.*, 29 EBC 1229 (N.D. Cal. 2002). The plaintiffs argued that the fiduciaries had three other options: (1) to sell the stock back to the company in a private transaction; (2) to seek an independent assessment from a financial or legal advisor, resign in favor of an independent fiduciary, or seek judicial guidance; and (3) to purchase insurance. The court rejected these alternatives. With respect to the first option, selling the stock back to the company, the court noted that the company was under no obligation to purchase the stock and that, for it to do so at the inflated predisclosure trading levels, would have shifted the loss to the company's other public shareholders. With respect to the second option, the court stated that retaining independent counsel or an outside fiduciary after learning of the accounting problems would not have avoided the plan losses and that an independent fiduciary would have been constrained by the same federal securities laws that applied to the defendant fiduciaries. Finally, the court stated that a purchase of insurance against the loss would not have solved the problem because the fiduciaries would have been obligated to disclose the accounting irregularities to the prospective insurer.

participants to hold and purchase additional shares of Enron stock. The Enron employees were given the right to direct the investment of the amounts credited to their retirement accounts, and one of the investments available to them was Enron stock. The defendants moved to dismiss this claim on the ground that they would have violated insider-trading rules under the federal securities laws if they had selectively disclosed only to the plan participants confidential information about accounting irregularities and financial improprieties at Enron, before this information was publicly disclosed, so that the ESOP participants could have made informed decisions regarding purchasing and holding Enron shares.

The court rejected this argument and adopted the position taken by the Department of Labor, in its amicus curiae brief, for resolving the alleged tension between ERISA and the federal securities laws. The Department of Labor argued that nothing in the securities laws would have prohibited the defendants from disclosing the information to other shareholders and to the public at large or from forcing Enron to do so. The court noted that if the inside information about Enron's precarious financial status had been made public by the plan fiduciaries, the price of the stock might have dropped before the plan participants could make a profit or reduce a substantial loss, but the damage to the plan participants then would not be the fault of the fiduciaries but rather of the underlying alleged fraudulent scheme and of the corporate officials who participated in it and who concealed it (and against whom the plan would have a cause of action). The court also noted that, as the Department of Labor argued, it would have been consistent with the securities laws for the administrative committee to have eliminated Enron stock as a participant investment option and as the employer match under Enron's Section 401(k) plan. Therefore, the court denied the defendants' motion to dismiss and ruled that the plan participants had stated a cause of action against the defendants for failure to disclose material inside information about Enron's financial status. The case then was settled out of court before a trial.[111]

---

111. *In re: Enron Corporation Securities Derivative & ERISA Litigation,* 204 F. Supp. 2d 511 (S.D. Tex. 2003) (discussed also in Question 15).

Q35 Does an employer have a duty to disclose information about proposed changes to an ESOP?

Yes. Once an employer begins serious consideration of a proposal to change the terms of an employee benefit plan covered by ERISA, it has an affirmative duty to disclose information about the proposal to all participants and beneficiaries to whom the employer knows, or has reason to know, that the information is material.[112] This affirmative duty of disclosure arises whether or not plan participants or beneficiaries have asked the employer for the information.[113] A proposal for a potential change in benefits is under "serious consideration" when a specific proposal is being discussed for purposes of implementation by senior management with the authority to implement the change.[114]

Q36 Must an ESOP fiduciary turn over a copy of the valuation report to a participant who requests to see it?

Section 104(b)(4) of ERISA provides as follows:

> The administrator shall, upon written request of any participant or beneficiary, furnish a copy of the latest updated summary plan description, and the latest annual report, any terminal report, the bargaining agreement, trust agreement, contract, or *other instruments under which the plan is established or operated*. (emphasis added)

The federal courts that have addressed the question whether an ESOP fiduciary is required to allow ESOP participants to see valuation reports have focused on the emphasized language and have disagreed regarding whether this language encompasses valuation reports. In a case decided in 1992, a California federal district court concluded that the valuation reports requested by participants in an ESOP were "instruments under which the plan was operated" and that participants in the plan therefore were entitled to see them.[115] There, the plaintiffs were plan participants who were questioning the accuracy of the computation of their benefits.

---

112. *Bins v. Exxon Co. U.S.A.*, 189 F.3d 929, 934 (9th Cir. 1999).
113. *Id.*
114. *Fischer v. Philadelphia Elec. Co.*, 96 F.3d 1533, 1539 (3d Cir. 1996).
115. *Werner v. Morgan Equipment Co.*, 1992 WL 453355 (N.D. Cal. 1992).

The court noted that the valuation report that the plaintiffs requested was specifically prepared to determine the price at which they would be able to sell the shares allocated to their ESOP accounts.

On the other hand, in a case decided in 1996, the Court of Appeals for the Fourth Circuit reached a contrary conclusion.[116] This court construed the language "other instruments under which the plan is established or operated" to mean the formal or legal documents under which a plan is set up or managed. The court noted that the ESOP was not set up or managed under the valuation reports and that hence the provisions of Section 104(b)(4) of ERISA do not encompass appraisal reports.

The Prudence Standard

Q37 What must a fiduciary do to satisfy the prudence requirement?

To satisfy the prudence requirement, a fiduciary must act "with the care, skill, prudence, and diligence under the circumstances then prevailing that a prudent man acting in a like capacity and familiar with such matters would use in the conduct of an enterprise of a like character and with like aims."[117]

Q38 What is the legal standard for determining whether a fiduciary's acts are prudent?

The standard for prudence depends on the circumstances. The scope of the fiduciary's duty of prudence is "limited to those factors and circumstances that a prudent person having similar duties and familiar with

---

116. *Faircloth v. Lundy Packing Co.*, 91 F.3d 648, 655 (4th Cir. 1996). *See also Board of Trustees of the CWA/ITU Negotiated Pension Plan v. Weinstein*, 107 F.3d 139 (2d Cir. 1997) (plan administrator not required to provide actuarial valuation reports to participants in the pension plan). *But see Bartling v. Fruehauf Corp.*, 29 F.3d 1062 (6th Cir. 1994) (plan administrator required to provide actuarial valuation reports to participants in a pension plan where the reports were required to be prepared under ERISA and therefore were "indispensable to the operation of the plan").

117. ERISA § 404(a)(1)(B).

such matters would consider relevant," whether the context is one of plan investments or otherwise.[118]

Q39 Are a fiduciary's actions judged by the standard of an ordinary person or that of an expert?

Particularly in the context of investing plan assets, a fiduciary charged with an investment decision must act as a prudent expert would act under similar circumstances, taking into account all relevant substantive factors, as they appeared at the time of the investment decision, not in hindsight. This standard under ERISA "is not that of a prudent lay person, but rather of a prudent fiduciary with experience dealing with a similar enterprise."[119]

Q40 What other standards do courts employ in determining whether an ESOP fiduciary has satisfied the prudence requirement?

In reviewing investment decisions made by fiduciaries of employee benefit plans, courts are concerned with the reasonableness of the decisions under the circumstances, not the ultimate results. The prudent-person standard is a test of how the fiduciary acted viewed from the perspective of the time of the challenged decision, rather than from the vantage point of hindsight.[120] As one federal court of appeals has stated, the fiduciary duty of care "requires prudence, not prescience."[121] Another

---

118. 44 Fed. Reg. 37,222–23 (June 25, 1979) (DOL release accompanying DOL Reg. § 2550.404a-1(b)).
119. *Whitfield v. Cohen*, 682 F. Supp. 188, 194 (S.D.N.Y. 1988), *quoting Marshall v. Snyder*, 1 EBC (BNA) 1878, 1886 (E.D.N.Y. 1979).
120. *Roth v. Sawyer-Cleator Lumber Co.*, 16 F.3d 915, 918 (8th Cir. 1994). *See also Katsaros v. Cody*, 744 F.2d 270, 279 (2d Cir. 1984), *cert. denied*, 469 U.S. 1072 (1984); *Armstrong v. Amsted Industries, Inc.*, 2004 WL 1745774 (N.D. Ill.), *rev'd on other grounds*, 446 F.3d 728 (7th Cir. 2006) (discussed in Question 29, Example 1, and Question 43); and *Metzler v. Graham*, 112 F.3d 207, 209 (5th Cir. 1997).
121. *DeBruyne v. Equitable Life Assurance Society*, 920 F.2d 457, 465 (7th Cir. 1990). *Accord, Keach v. U.S. Trust Co., N.A.*, 419 F.3d 626 (7th Cir. 2005) (discussed in Question 111).

federal court has stated that the court's responsibility in evaluating the conduct of trustees whose actions are challenged is to determine how a "hypothetical prudent fiduciary" would have reacted if faced with the circumstances presented in the case before the court.[122]

Q41 How does the prudence requirement apply with respect to voting stock of the sponsoring employer?

The Department of Labor has taken the position that the voting of proxies is a fiduciary act of plan asset management.[123] Therefore, according to the Department of Labor, ERISA fiduciaries must act for the exclusive purpose of providing benefits to plan participants and in a prudent manner in voting shares of stock that they hold. The responsibility for voting proxies lies exclusively with the plan trustee, unless the plan provides that the trustee is subject to the direction of a named fiduciary or unless the power to manage assets has been delegated to an investment manager. In voting proxies, a responsible fiduciary should consider those factors that may affect the value of the plan's investment and must not subordinate the interests of the participants and beneficiaries in their retirement income to unrelated objectives.

Q42 Should an ESOP fiduciary monitor or seek to influence the management of the plan sponsor?

It is appropriate for ERISA fiduciaries to monitor or influence the management of corporations in which their plans own stock where the fiduciaries conclude that "there is a reasonable expectation that such monitoring or communication with management, by the plan alone or together with other shareholders, is likely to enhance the value of the plan's investment in the corporation, after taking into account the costs involved."[124] According to the Department of Labor, a reasonable expectation that monitoring or influencing corporate management is likely to enhance

---

122. *Kuper v. Quantum Chemicals Corp.*, 852 F. Supp. 1389, 1397 (S.D. Oh 1994), aff'd sub nom. *Kuper v. Iovenko*, 66 F.3d 1447 (6th Cir. 1995) (discussed in Question 55, Example 2).
123. DOL Interp. Bull. No. 94-2, 59 F.R. 38860 (July 29, 1994).
124. *Id.*

the value of the plan's investment may exist where plan investments in corporate stock are held as long-term investments, as typically is true in the case of an ESOP, or where a plan may not be able to easily dispose of the corporate stock, as is generally the case where an ESOP is sponsored by the corporation whose stock is not publicly traded. Issues with respect to which the Department of Labor believes that ERISA trustees should actively monitor the activities of management include the following:

- the independence and expertise of candidates for the plan sponsor's board of directors;
- assuring that the plan sponsor's board of directors has sufficient information to carry out its responsibility to monitor the performance of management;
- the appropriateness of executive compensation;
- the plan sponsor's policy regarding mergers and acquisitions;
- the extent of the plan sponsor's debt financing and its capitalization in general;
- the nature of the plan sponsor's long-term business plan;
- the plan sponsor's investment in training to develop its workforce;
- other workplace practices; and
- financial and other measures of corporate performance.[125]

While there are many areas with respect to which ERISA trustees should actively monitor the actions and decisions of the officers and directors of the plan sponsor, ESOP trustees are *not* required to independently evaluate business transactions properly authorized by corporate management. ERISA fiduciaries are not corporate fiduciaries, and it is not the responsibility of an ESOP trustee to second-guess the business decisions of the plan sponsor's management.[126] As discussed above in Question

---

125. *Id.*
126. *Kuper v. Iovenko*, 66 F.3d 1447, 1460 (6th Cir. 1995) (ESOP fiduciaries did not breach their duties by failing to block the plan sponsor's decision to transfer ESOP assets from one trust to another) (discussed in Question 55, Example 2); *Martin v. Feilen*, 965 F.2d 660, 666 (8th Cir. 1992), *cert. denied*, 113 S. Ct.

19, the shares of a plan sponsor's stock held by an ESOP are assets of the plan, but the properties owned by the plan sponsor are not plan assets.[127] Therefore, the conduct and management of the plan sponsor's business is not a matter of ERISA fiduciary responsibility.[128]

Q43 How does the prudence requirement apply with respect to forecasting an ESOP company's repurchase obligation?

An ESOP sponsored by a corporation whose shares are not readily tradable on a national securities exchange generally must provide that a participant who is entitled to receive a distribution from the plan may demand that his or her benefits be distributed in the form of stock of the employer. In that case, the participant also must be given a put option to sell the stock to the plan sponsor.[129] That is, the participants must have the right to require the employer, *not* the ESOP, to repurchase any employer stock distributed to them, using a "fair valuation formula."[130] This is generally referred to as an ESOP company's "repurchase liability" or "repurchase obligation." Although this liability or obligation is a liability or obligation of the company which sponsors the ESOP, not of the ESOP trust, one federal court has held that ESOP fiduciaries have a duty to prudently manage

---

979 (1993) (although an employer's business decisions affect the value of its stock and thus the benefits under an ESOP that it sponsors, ESOP fiduciaries do not become liable for these decisions) (discussed in Question 27, Example 1); and *Armstrong v. Amsted Industries, Inc.*, 2004 WL 1745774 (N.D. Ill.) *rev'd on other grounds*, 446 F.3d 728 (7th Cir. 2006) (ESOP trustee was not obligated to conduct an independent investigation of a proposed acquisition of another corporation by the plan sponsor) (discussed in Question 29, Example 1, and in Question 43).

127. DOL Regs. § 2510.3-101(a)(2).
128. DOL Regs. § 2510.3-101(a), (c), and (h)(3).
129. Code § 409(h). There are two exceptions to this general rule. ESOP participants may be required to take their benefits in the form of cash when either (1) the plan sponsor has made the election to be treated as an S corporation for federal income tax purposes, or (2) the charter or bylaws of the plan sponsor require that substantially all of the outstanding shares of the plan sponsor must be held by employees or by an employee benefit trust. Code § 409(h)(2)(B).
130. Code § 409(h)(1)(B).

the plan sponsor's repurchase obligation.[131] However, as discussed above in Question 40, the prudence of a fiduciary's actions must be evaluated from the perspective of the time of his or her actions, and not with the benefit of hindsight. Therefore, the court held that the mere fact that a plan sponsor's repurchase liability forecasts are erroneous, even seriously erroneous, is not sufficient to establish imprudence.

> ***Example.*** During its fiscal year that ended September 30, 2000, Amsted Industries, Inc., a 100% ESOP-owned company, incurred a share repurchase cost far in excess of what it had projected for that year. During that year, Amsted suffered from a downturn in all of the markets in which it conducted business operations, and its profits declined substantially. The value of its outstanding shares declined from $184.41 per share as of September 30, 1999, to $89.87 per share as of September 30, 2000. During fiscal year 2000, an unprecedented number of employees of Amsted left the company. Participants in Amsted's ESOP brought a class action against Amsted, members of Amsted's ESOP committee, two vice-presidents of Amsted, and the trustee of Amsted's ESOP, alleging, among other things, that the fiduciaries breached their fiduciary duties by failing to properly monitor Amsted's repurchase obligation.
>
> Amsted forecasted its anticipated repurchase obligations on an annual basis as part of its normal business-planning process, and it used available computer software to help in the analysis of its repurchase obligation. Even though the fiduciaries' repurchase obligation estimates for fiscal year 2000 were substantially below the actual obligation, the court found that their actions did not constitute imprudence. The court noted that the two primary factors identified by the plaintiffs' repurchase obligation expert to be taken into account in a repurchase-liability analysis—the historical share turnover rate and employee attitudes toward the ESOP—would not have shown that the defendants should have predicted a redemption rate of over 30% during fiscal year 2000 (up from between 9 and 9.4% for the preceding two years). The court also noted that the defendants'

---

131. *Armstrong v. Amsted Industries, Inc.*, 2004 WL 1745774 (N.D. Ill. 2004) *rev'd on other grounds*, 446 F.3d 728 (7th Cir. 2006) (discussed also in Question 29, Example 1).

financial expert performed a statistical survey that showed that there was less than a 1% probability that the fiscal year 2000 turnover rate would have occurred. Moreover, Amsted had a substantial amount of unused availability on its bank credit facility, and the court found no evidence that even the most prudent of fiduciaries would have determined that this cash cushion would not be sufficient to satisfy the company's repurchase obligation.[132]

Q44 What role should an ESOP fiduciary play in determining the appropriateness of executive compensation?

Executive compensation policies should be set by a corporation's board of directors. It is a good practice for the board to approve a specific plan, including objective criteria, to determine officers' compensation. Factors that are appropriate to take into account in a compensation plan include company profitability, other performance goals, and industry standards. An ESOP fiduciary should monitor the policies adopted and actions taken by the board of directors with respect to executive compensation.

Ideally, officers' compensation should be set by a compensation committee composed of outside directors. It is advisable for an ESOP company to arrange for independent persons to serve on its board of directors, both for purposes of approving officers' compensation and for reviewing other transactions with respect to which inside directors may have conflicts of interest. Where an ESOP company has no outside directors, consideration should be given to retaining independent compensation consultants to provide the company with objective counseling regarding appropriate types and levels of officer compensation. In addition, fairness opinions from independent compensation consultants should be obtained in connection with the declaration of extraordinary bonuses or the implementation of any significant deferred or equity compensation programs. This is especially important where corporate officers are serving as the ESOP trustees. They should not be in a position to unilaterally set their own compensation.

Example. During the years 1989–1994, Andrew W. Patton served as the president of Delta Star, Inc. In addition he was a trustee of the

---

132. *Id.*

company's ESOP, which held 98.6% of the company's outstanding shares. During his tenure as president of Delta Star, Patton unilaterally determined increases in base salaries for all senior managers, including himself. Between 1989 and 1994, he increased his own base salary from approximately $200,000 to approximately $300,000, and he awarded himself annual bonuses that averaged approximately $450,000 and that exceeded $1 million in 1991. Patton also arranged for the company to adopt two deferred compensation plans that provided very large benefits for him. Although the company's net sales varied significantly during the years 1989–1994, its yearly net income remained relatively flat due to the fact that excess revenues were paid out to key managers in the form of salary increases and bonuses.

The procedure by which Patton arranged for the payment of bonuses to himself and to others never was approved by the board of directors of Delta Star. In fact, Patton took steps to conceal the amounts of the bonuses paid to senior managers from the other officers of the company, from the other members of the board of directors, and from the other ESOP trustees. There were no formal documents that laid out the criteria which Patton considered in determining bonus amounts, and no predetermined targets or performance goals for bonuses were established.

After Patton's retirement, the board of directors of Delta Star authorized a lawsuit against him seeking reimbursement of excessive compensation. The court ruled that Patton had violated his fiduciary duties, both as a director of the company and as an ESOP trustee. The court stated that Patton either should have recused himself in connection with consideration of his own compensation or resigned as an ESOP trustee. The court held that Patton breached his fiduciary duties by failing to conduct an independent investigation into the self-dealing acts that he took as an officer and director of the company. The court found that Patton's self-dealing resulted in a diminution in the value of the company stock held by the ESOP, and the court ordered him to repay all salary increases and bonuses that he awarded himself in excess of his original base salary. The court also required Patton to forfeit his rights under the deferred compensation plans.[133]

---

133. *Delta Star, Inc. v. Patton*, 76 F. Supp. 2d 617 (W.D. Pa. 1999).

Q45 Can an ESOP fiduciary avoid liability for an imprudent decision by establishing that he or she acted in good faith?

No. Case law establishes that the conduct of ESOP fiduciaries must be measured by objective standards and that a good-faith belief on the part of the fiduciaries that their actions were in the best interests of the plan participants is not sufficient to absolve them of liability for imprudent actions.[134] As one court has stated, "[a] fiduciary's *independent* investigation of the merits of a particular investment is at the heart of the prudent person standard."[135]

Q46 What is the standard of review applied by courts in evaluating the prudence of the conduct of an independent ESOP fiduciary?

Judicial review of the actions of independent ESOP fiduciaries is highly deferential. As one federal court of appeals has stated, the decisions of an independent fiduciary will be upheld "unless they are arbitrary and capricious, not supported by substantial evidence or erroneous on a question of law."[136]

Example. An independent ESOP trustee purchased stock of the sponsoring employer at the direction of the plan administrator, which

---

134. *Donovan v. Bierwirth*, 538 F. Supp. 463, 470 (E.D.N.Y. 1981), *aff'd*, 680 F.2d 263 (2d Cir. 1982) ("a belief, even a good faith belief, held by the trustees does not insulate them from charges that they have acted imprudently") (discussed in Question 49, Example 1, and Question 122). *See also Donovan v. Cunningham*, 716 F.2d 1455 (5th Cir. 1983), *cert. denied*, 467 U.S. 1251 (1984) (discussed in Question 106, Example 1).

135. *Whitfield v. Cohen*, 682 F. Supp. 188, 194 (S.D.N.Y. 1988) (emphasis added). *Accord, Reich v. Valley Nat'l. Bank of Arizona*, 837 F. Supp. 1259 (S.D.N.Y. 1993) (discussed in Question 49, Example 2, and in Question 51).

136. *Armstrong v. Amsted Industries, Inc.*, 446 F.3d 728 (7th Cir. 2006) (discussed in Question 29, Example 1, and in Question 43); *Ershick v. United Missouri Bank of Kansas City*, 948 F.2d 660, 666 (10th Cir. 1991). *Kuper v. Iovenko*, 66 F.3d 1447 (6th Cir. 1995) (discussed in Question 55, Example 2); and *Moench v. Robertson*, 62 F.3d 553 (3d Cir. 1995) (discussed in Question 55, Example 1).

was the sponsoring employer. The plan document provided that the administrator had the power to direct the trustee with regard to purchases of company stock. The trustee purchased company stock following the death of the founder of the company, after which the sponsoring employer's fortunes declined precipitously. The purchase prices paid by the trustee for the stock were determined by an independent appraiser. Former employees of the sponsoring employer, whose ESOP account balances had declined by 75% of their former values, alleged that the trustee had violated ERISA by imprudently investing in employer stock during the time when the financial condition of the sponsoring employer was deteriorating and by failing to attempt to sell some or all of the employer stock. The court held that the trustee had not violated ERISA. It found that the decline in the price of the employer's stock occurred over a year after the trustee made its last purchase, and it held that this was insufficient to show imprudence on the part of the trustee.[137]

Q47 What is the standard of review applied by courts in evaluating the prudence of the conduct of an ESOP fiduciary who has a conflict of interest?

Where an ESOP fiduciary has a conflict of interest, courts will apply a higher standard in reviewing his or her conduct than in cases involving independent fiduciaries. As one court has stated, when a fiduciary has dual loyalties, his or her independent investigation into the basis for an investment decision which presents a potential conflict of interest must be "both intensive and scrupulous and must be discharged with the greatest degree of care that could be expected under all the circumstances by reasonable beneficiaries and participants of the plan."[138] Application of this standard of review generally results in a detailed examination by

---

137. *Ershick v. United Missouri Bank of Kansas City*, 948 F.2d 6610, 668 (10th Cir. 1991).

138. *Donovan v. Bierwirth*, 538 F. Supp. 463, 470 (E.D.N.Y. 1981), *aff'd*, 680 F.2d 263 (2d Cir. 1982) (discussed in Question 49, Example 1, and in Question 122). *Accord, Moench v. Robertson*, 62 F.3d 553 (3d Cir. 1995) (discussed in Question 55, Example 1); *Martin v. Feilen*, 965 F.2d 660, 670 (8th Cir. 1992), *cert. denied*, 113 S.Ct. 979 (1993) (discussed in Question 27, Example 1).

the court of the extent of the fiduciary's investigation and evaluation of a challenged investment or act.[139]

Q48 What is the difference between "substantive prudence" and "procedural prudence"?

The Department of Labor and some courts and commentators have distinguished between two types of prudence: substantive prudence and procedural prudence. The former refers to the merits of the decision made by the fiduciary; the latter addresses the process through which the fiduciary reaches his or her decision. Courts examine both the process used by the fiduciary to reach a decision as well as the merits of the decision.[140] As long as there is no conflict of interest that would impair the fiduciary's exercise of independent judgment, a fiduciary who considers the appropriate substantive factors ("substantive prudence") and does so using proper procedures ("procedural prudence") will satisfy the prudence requirement.[141]

---

139. *Moench v. Robertson*, 62 F.3d 553, 572 (3d Cir. 1995) (claim that failure by ESOP trustees, who also were directors of the plan sponsor, to invest ESOP funds in properties other than stock of the plan sponsor when that stock was rapidly declining in value stated a cause of action) (discussed in Question 55, Example 1); *Martin v. Feilen*, 965 F.2d 660, 670 (8th Cir. 1992), *cert. denied*, 113 S.Ct. 979 (1993) (when a fiduciary has dual loyalties, the prudence standard requires that he or she make a careful and impartial investigation of all investment decisions) (discussed in Question 27, Example 1). *See also Horn v. McQueen*, 215 F. Supp. 2d 867, 875 (W.D. Ky. 2002) (discussed in Question 106, Example 3), where the court applied a "prudent person standard" in evaluating the conduct of ESOP trustees who were accused of paying an excessive price for shares of the plan sponsor in order to retain control of the company. In this case, the court appears to have confused the concept of a standard of judicial review of fiduciary conduct with the concept of a standard of conduct applicable to ESOP fiduciaries. The court could have avoided this confusion by rejecting the defendants' attempt to invoke the "arbitrary and capricious" standard on the ground that this standard applies only to judicial review of the conduct of independent fiduciaries.

140. *Eyler v. Comm'r.*, 88 F.3d 445 (7th Cir. 1996) (discussed in Question 106, Example 2); and *Donovan v. Cunningham*, 716 F.2d 1455 (5th Cir. 1983), *cert. denied*, 467 U.S. 1251 (1984) (discussed in Question 106, Example 1).

141. *Katsaros v. Cody*, 744 F.2d 270, 279 (2d Cir), *cert. denied*, 469 U.S. 1072 (1984).

Q49 What constitutes procedural prudence?

Employee benefit plan fiduciaries have a duty to investigate the investments they administer. As one federal court of appeals has stated, a court's task in evaluating the prudence of a fiduciary's conduct is to inquire "whether the individual trustees, at the time they engaged in the challenged transactions, employed the appropriate methods to investigate the merits of the investment and to structure the investment."[142] In applying this and similar standards in ERISA prudence cases, the courts have held that the fiduciary's conduct must be measured by objective standards and that a good-faith belief by the trustees that their actions are in the best interests of the plan participants is not sufficient.

> *Example 1.* The trustees of a pension plan sponsored by a public corporation for whose shares a tender offer had been made declined to tender the shares held in the plan and used pension assets to purchase additional shares of the plan sponsor in the open market. At the same time, the plan trustees, who also were officers and directors of the company, led a vigorous fight against the tender offer. The court found that the trustees had breached their fiduciary duties by failing to take appropriate precautions to protect the interests of the participants in the plan in light of the trustees' conflict of interest and by failing to adequately consider the merits of the tender offer. The court found that the trustees had conducted no real inquiry into the dangers presented to the pension plan by the takeover proposal. Rather, the court found that the trustees spent all of their time looking for ways to fight the tender offer and that their conduct was motivated solely by their desire to defeat the offer. The court noted that the trustees failed to consider how the pension plan, as opposed to the plan sponsor, might have benefited by tendering its shares of the plan sponsor or how the pension plan might have been protected in the case of a successful takeover bid. The court also noted that the trustees failed to consult with outside, independent counsel or with

---

142. *Donovan v. Mazzola*, 716 F.2d 1226, 1232 (9th Cir. 1983), *cert. denied*, 104 S.Ct. 704 (1984). *See also Fink v. National Sav. and Trust Co.*, 772 F.2d 951, 955 (D.C. Cir. 1985); and *Katsaros v. Cody*, 744 F.2d 270, 279 (2d Cir 1984), *cert. denied*, 469 U.S. 1072 (1984).

an independent investment adviser. The court held that the violation by the trustees of their duty to investigate was an independent basis for imposing liability upon them under ERISA.[143]

Example 2. In December 1986, the officers of Kroy, Inc., took their company private in a management-led leveraged buyout. In order to finance the transaction, Kroy created an ESOP that purchased $35.5 million dollars worth of Kroy shares. From 1987 through 1990, Kroy contributed $17.5 million to the ESOP, which funds were used to repay the ESOP loan. After the transaction, Kroy's sales and earnings declined drastically, and in 1990 Kroy declared bankruptcy. In December 1989, the Department of Labor brought an action against Valley National Bank of Arizona, the ESOP trustee, alleging that Valley had breached its fiduciary duties under ERISA by, among other things, failing to conduct a good-faith independent investigation of the transaction and by permitting the ESOP to purchase the Kroy shares at a price in excess of fair market value.

Valley accepted its appointment as ESOP trustee on December 16, 1986. At that time, the transaction was scheduled to close on December 18, 1986. At the request of another investor, the transaction was postponed until December 23, 1986. Before December 16, three officers of Kroy had been serving as the trustees, but they resigned because of difficulties in obtaining fiduciary liability insurance. The price for the shares to be purchased by the ESOP was determined by Banker's Trust Company, which had been retained by the company to determine the feasibility of an ESOP transaction. Before accepting appointment as trustee, Valley had been invited to participate in the financing for the transaction. Valley declined to participate as a lender because it had determined that Kroy's declining sales and profitability rendered it unlikely that Kroy could service the debt that it would incur as a result of the ESOP transaction.

Valley had never before served as a trustee in connection with a multi-investor ESOP transaction, and the trust officer who acted on behalf of Valley, Russell Gunderson, was a salesperson who had no experience reviewing stock valuations. The only documents that

---

143. *Donovan v. Bierwirth*, 538 F. Supp. 463 (E.D.N.Y. 1981), *aff'd*, 680 F.2d 263 (2d Cir. 1982). The damages aspect of this case is discussed in Question 122.

Gunderson reviewed before Valley's acceptance of its appointment as the ESOP trustee were the ESOP plan documents and a copy of the company's proxy statement. He reviewed the valuation report for the first time on December 16th. Although Gunderson testified that he read the report, he acknowledged that he did not review the report page-by-page with the appraiser, but instead discussed it in general terms only. Gunderson also testified that instead of making an independent analysis, he relied upon the assurances supplied by the appraiser. In its opinion, the court noted that Gunderson never discussed with the original trustees their opinion about the transaction, he did not visit Kroy's plant, he never read relevant corporate governance documents, he never interviewed Kroy management, and he did not attempt to undertake any negotiations with the company on behalf of the ESOP.

The court granted summary judgment in favor of the Department of Labor. The court stated that in order for Valley to prevail, it had to prove that it arrived at its determination of the fair market value of the Kroy stock by way of a prudent investigation under the circumstances then prevailing. In holding that Valley failed to establish that it conducted a prudent investigation, the court noted that Valley failed to take any independent steps to evaluate the transaction and failed to understand the basis for and the evidence used to create the valuation report. The court found that, in essence, all that Valley did was come in to a transaction whose closing was imminent and close the transaction. The court imposed a judgment against Valley in the amount of $17.5 million.[144]

Example 3. In 1984, senior executives of Parsons Corporation arranged for an ESOP to participate in a leveraged buyout of all of Parsons Corporation's outstanding stock, which was publicly held. The ESOP became the sole shareholder of Parsons. Participants in the ESOP brought a class action against Parsons; members of the board of directors of Parsons; senior executives of Parsons; and members of the Retirement Committee, which was the named fiduciary of the ESOP. The plaintiffs alleged that the defendants breached their fiduciary duties by approving the leveraged buyout. The terms of

---

144. *Reich v. Valley Nat'l. Bank of Arizona*, 837 F. Supp. 1259 (S.D.N.Y. 1993).

the buyout were negotiated between the Retirement Committee, a special committee created to represent the interests of the public shareholders in the transaction, and Parsons, which made the loan to the ESOP to enable it to purchase the Parsons shares tendered pursuant to the buyout. Parsons management recommended financial and legal advisors for the Retirement Committee. The Retirement Committee interviewed and evaluated these firms before deciding to retain them. The financial and legal advisors were well-known firms with extensive experience in ERISA matters. The purchase price for the Parsons stock was determined by negotiations between Parsons, the Retirement Committee, and the special committee.

All three members of the Retirement Committee testified that they were informed repeatedly of their fiduciary obligations to the ESOP participants, that they understood these obligations, and that they believed that they had performed in accordance with these fiduciary duties. The court was strongly and favorably impressed with the character, confidence, and integrity of each member of the Committee and found their testimony to be credible. The court found that the Retirement Committee evaluated the transaction thoroughly on behalf of the ESOP participants. In support of this conclusion, the court noted that the Committee had retained independent and competent legal and financial advisors to assist in the decision-making process, had considered the potential short-term disadvantages of the leveraged buyout, and had negotiated mechanisms for minimizing these disadvantages. In particular, they negotiated for the establishment of a "floor price," pursuant to which individuals who retired during the period when the per-share value of the stock was reduced by reason of the ESOP indebtedness would receive a specified minimum amount for their shares. In addition, the accounts of the participants in the ESOP were restored to their pre-transaction account value through additions of newly issued shares to their accounts by means of a bargain sale. Based on these facts, the court concluded that the members of the Retirement Committee had acted prudently and dismissed the plaintiffs' claims.[145]

---

145. *Andrade v. Parsons Corp.*, 12 EBC (BNA) 1954 (C.D. Ca. 1990), *aff'd*, 1992 U.S. App. LEXIS 18220 (9th Cir. 1992).

Q50 Does an ESOP fiduciary have an obligation to seek the assistance of an expert to satisfy the prudence requirement?

Yes. It is not possible for an individual ESOP fiduciary to be an expert in all phases of ESOP administration, and no single ESOP fiduciary can have knowledge of the entire range of activities involved in the operation of an ESOP. Therefore, ESOP fiduciaries have an affirmative duty to seek the advice and counsel of independent experts when their own knowledge is insufficient under the circumstances. For example, ESOP trustees must retain independent financial advisors to assist them in determining whether to purchase or sell stock of the sponsoring employer. See Question 107. In addition, ESOP trustees should retain independent legal counsel to advise them regarding how to satisfy their legal responsibilities. See Question 111. Where the ESOP trustee is a bank or a trust company, it may have business appraisers, lawyers, and other experts on staff, in which case it would not be necessary to retain outside advisors.

Q51 Will an ESOP fiduciary be absolved of liability if he or she acts in reliance upon the advice of a qualified independent adviser?

One of the most effective actions that an ESOP fiduciary can take to protect himself or herself when confronted with a difficult decision is to obtain advice from independent experts, especially where the fiduciaries have conflicting interests. However, ESOP fiduciaries cannot rely solely upon the advice of outside advisors. Rather, ESOP fiduciaries must exercise their own judgment, taking into account the advice of their legal, financial, and other advisors. Merely engaging outside advisors and following their advice, without more, will not operate as a complete whitewash that satisfies the ERISA prudence requirement.

In relying upon the advice of outside experts, ERISA fiduciaries have a responsibility to evaluate the advice that is presented and to make sure that they understand it. Among other things, ESOP fiduciaries should verify that their advisors have obtained all necessary or appropriate information, that their assumptions are valid, and that their recommendations make sense in light of the relevant facts and circumstances.[146] For a more detailed discussion regarding the extent to which ESOP fiduciaries can rely upon business valuation reports, see Question 110.

> *Example.* The ESOP trustee that participated in the leveraged buyout of Kroy, Inc., which went bankrupt within four years of the transaction (and which transaction is described in the second example under Question 49), sought to defend the prudence of its stock purchase, in part, by reliance upon a legal opinion that the ESOP transaction did not violate ERISA. However, the legal opinion was based on the assumption that a flawed valuation report was valid and ignored the duty of the trustee to independently assess the validity of the valuation report. The legal opinion also recited that the trustee had determined that the purchase price was fair and that the proposed stock purchase was prudent and in the best interests of the plan participants. The court concluded that the legal opinion did not constitute approval of the proposed transaction. Moreover, the court held that the trustee could not rely on the advice of its legal counsel because the trustee had failed to perform the tasks that its legal counsel had directed it to perform, including a review of the terms and interest rate of the proposed ESOP loan and a careful review of the valuation report.[147]

Q52 Can a trustee be held liable for an imprudent resignation?

Yes. Under traditional trust law, a trustee is permitted to resign in accordance with the terms of the trust, with the consent of the beneficiaries

---

146. *See, e.g., Howard v. Shay*, 100 F.3d 1484 (9th Cir. 1996) (improper reliance upon an appraisal report) (discussed at Q110, Example 1); and *Reich v. Valley Nat'l. Bank of Arizona*, 837 F. Supp. 1259 (S.D.N.Y. 1993) (improper reliance upon legal opinion and valuation report) (discussed in Question 49, Example 2). *See also Roth v. Sawyer-Cleator Lumber Co*, 16 F.3d 915, at 918–19 (8th Cir. 1994).

147. *Reich v. Valley Nat'l. Bank of Arizona*, 837 F. Supp. 1259 (S.D.N.Y. 1993).

of the trust, or with a court's permission.[148] An ESOP trust agreement typically sets forth a procedure by which the trustee may resign. Typically, the trust agreement requires a trustee to provide the plan sponsor with reasonable advance notice of its intent to resign, during which time the plan sponsor can identify and designate a successor trustee. The resigning trustee then typically is required to transfer the employer securities and other plan assets to the new trustee. The resigning trustee's obligations are terminated when adequate provision has been made for the continued prudent management of the plan assets. However, a trustee may be liable for breach of fiduciary duty for resigning without providing for a suitable and trustworthy replacement.[149]

> **Example.** Jeffrey Ream brought an action against Fulton Bank for breach of fiduciary responsibility in connection with the bank's resignation as the trustee of a profit-sharing plan sponsored by Ream's employer, JLC Construction Company. The company failed to provide the bank with employer matching contributions required under the terms of the plan for the years 1992 and 1993. The bank sent letters to the company demanding payment of the past-due amounts, but received no response. The bank then sent a letter to the company's president and sole shareholder, Jeffrey Frey, stating that it was resigning as trustee pursuant to the terms of the plan. The bank requested the appointment of a successor trustee, but Frey never responded and a successor trustee never was appointed. Finally, the bank delivered the plan assets to Frey and appointed him as the successor trustee. Frey subsequently converted all of the plan assets to his own use. In 1994, the company declared bankruptcy.
>
> Ream brought an action against the bank to recover the balance that had been credited to his account under the terms of the plan. The court held that the bank had breached its fiduciary duties because it made no effort to ensure the continued viability of the plan after its resignation. The court noted that the bank was aware that the company

---

148. Restatement of the Law (Second) Trusts § 106. *See Glaziers and Glassworkers Union Local No. 252 Annuity Fund v. Newbridge Secs., Inc.*, 93 F.3d 1171, 1183–84 (3d Cir. 1996).

149. *Friend v. Sanwa Bank California*, 35 F.3d 466, 471 (9th Cir. 1994) (concurring opinion).

was having financial difficulties in that it had failed to make required contributions to the plan. According to the court, this knowledge, combined with Frey's failure to respond to the bank's numerous attempts to communicate about the future administration of the plan, should have led the bank to recognize that turning over the assets to Frey posed a real threat to the plan assets. The court concluded that the bank failed to act prudently in sending the plan assets to Frey and failing to inform plan beneficiaries of the circumstances. While the court stated that the bank was not required to remain as plan trustee, it ruled that the bank could not appoint Frey as the successor trustee and turn over the assets to him, at least without giving the plan beneficiaries reasonable advance notice, which would have given them an opportunity to take steps to protect the plan assets.[150]

Diversification

Q53 What is required for a fiduciary to satisfy the ERISA diversification requirement?

A fiduciary must diversify plan investments so as to minimize the risk of large losses unless, under the circumstances, it is clearly prudent not to do so.[151] However, in the case of an ESOP or other eligible individual account plan, the diversification requirement is not violated by the acquisition or holding of qualifying employer securities.[152] (See the discussion of qualifying employer securities in Question 85.)

Q54 If an ESOP holds assets in addition to employer stock, do the diversification rules apply?

Yes. Although an ESOP, by definition, is designed to invest *primarily* in stock of the sponsoring employer, and may invest solely in stock of the sponsoring employer, an ESOP also may invest in other assets. To the extent that the assets of an ESOP trust are comprised of assets other than qualifying employer securities, the general ERISA diversification rule

---

150. *Ream v. Frey*, 107 F.3d 147, 156, (3d Cir. 1997).
151. ERISA § 404(a)(1)(C).
152. ERISA § 404(a)(2).

applies. In addition, and notwithstanding that an ESOP is designed to invest primarily in qualifying employer securities, there may be situations where, because of declining fortunes of the sponsoring employer, an ESOP fiduciary should seek to sell employer securities held by the plan and diversify the assets of the plan. See Question 55.

Q55 Are there any other circumstances under which an ESOP fiduciary has a duty to diversify plan assets?

As one federal court of appeals has stated, "under normal circumstances, ESOP fiduciaries cannot be taken to task for failing to diversify investments, regardless of how prudent diversification would be under the terms of an ordinary non-ESOP pension plan."[153] This result derives both from the fact that ESOPs, by definition, are designed to invest primarily in employer securities and from the fact that ERISA specifically provides that an ESOP (or other eligible individual account plan) will not violate the ERISA diversification requirement merely by acquiring or holding qualifying employer securities. Many courts have recognized that, unlike pension plans, ESOPs are not intended to guarantee retirement benefits and, by their very nature, place employee retirement assets at much greater risk than typical diversified ERISA plans.[154]

Although employee ownership is recognized both in ERISA and by the courts as a goal to be served by ESOPs, the courts also have noted that ESOPs are covered by ERISA's stringent requirements and that, notwithstanding the general exemption from the diversification requirement, ESOP fiduciaries must act in accordance with the duties of loyalty and care embodied in the exclusive benefit and prudence rules. This makes it difficult to delineate the responsibilities of ESOP trustees where the value of the employer securities held by an ESOP is declining significantly. As one court has stated, in these circumstances ESOP trustees "must satisfy

---

153. *Moench v. Robertson*, 62 F.3d 553, 568 (3d Cir. 1995).
154. *E.g., Moench v. Robertson*, 62 F3d 553, 568 (3d Cir. 1995); *Martin v. Feilen*, 965 F2d 660, 664 (8th Cir. 1992), *cert. denied*, 113 S. Ct. 979 (1993) (discussed in Question 27, Example 1); and *Donovan v. Cunningham*, 716 F.2d 1455, 1466 (5th Cir. 1983) *cert. denied*, 467 S. Ct. 1251 (1984) (discussed in Question 106, Example 1).

the demands of Congressional policies that seem destined to collide."[155] As this court went on to explain:

> On the one hand, Congress has repeatedly expressed its intent to encourage the formation of ESOPs by passing legislation granting such plans favorable treatment, and has warned against judicial and administrative action that would thwart that goal. Competing with Congress' expressed policy to foster the formation of ESOPs is the policy expressed in equally forceful terms in ERISA: that of safeguarding the interests of participants in employee benefit plans by vigorously enforcing standards of fiduciary responsibility.[156]

Courts generally have sought to reconcile these competing policies by holding that an ESOP fiduciary who invests the plan assets in employer stock is entitled to a presumption that it has acted properly, but that plan participants or others challenging the trustee's investment decisions may overcome that presumption by establishing that the trustee abused its discretion.[157]

---

155. *Donovan v. Cunningham*, 716 F.2d 1455, 1466 (5th Cir. 1983) (footnotes omitted), *cert. denied*, 467 U.S. 1251 (1984) (discussed in Question 106, Example 1).
156. *Id.*
157. *Moench v. Robertson*, 62 F.3d 553, 571 (3d Cir. 1995). *Accord, Kuper v. Iovenko*, 66 F.3d 1447, 1459 (6th Cir. 1995) ("a proper balance between the purpose of ERISA and the nature of ESOPs requires that we review an ESOP fiduciary's decision to invest in employer securities for an abuse of discretion") (discussed in Example 2). Two federal courts have questioned the prudence standard established by *Moench* and have suggested that a more appropriate interpretation of the law might be that there can be no claim for breach of fiduciary duty arising out of a failure to diversify, but neither court found it necessary to reevaluate the *Moench* standard because they found that the claims of the plaintiffs in those cases failed under that standard. *Wright v. Oregon Metallurgical Corp.*, 360 F.3d 1090, 1097 (9th Cir. 2004) (stating that "the Third Circuit's intermediate prudence standard is difficult to reconcile with ERISA's statutory text, which exempts [eligible individual account plans] from the prudence requirement to the extent that it requires diversification" and suggesting that the statutory language exempting eligible individual account plans from the diversification requirement may be absolute, so that the prudence requirement cannot be read to support even an "albeit tempered duty to diversify") (discussed in Example 3); and *In re: McKesson HBOC ERISA Lit.*, 29 EBC 1229 at 5 (N.D. Cal. 2002) (unpublished opinion) ("If there is no duty to diversify ESOP plan assets under the statute, it logically follows that there can be no claim for breach of fidu-

Example 1. A former employee of Statewide Bancorp, who participated in the bank's ESOP, brought an action against members of the ESOP committee, alleging that they breached their fiduciary duties by failing to diversify the ESOP trust fund during the period that the value of the bank's stock declined drastically. The bank began experiencing financial difficulties in 1989. Between July 1989 and December 1989, the market value of its stock fell from $18.20 per share to $9.50 per share. The value declined to $6.00 per share in July 1990, to $2.25 per share in December 1990, and finally to less than $.25 per share by May 1991. During this period, federal regulatory authorities repeatedly expressed concerns to the bank's board of directors over problems with the bank's portfolio and financial condition. Overruling a grant of summary judgment for the defendants by the trial court, the court of appeals held that the plaintiff had stated a claim upon which he was entitled to a trial. The court stated that although an ESOP fiduciary who invests in stock of the sponsoring employer is entitled to a presumption that he or she has acted consistently with ERISA, this presumption may be overcome by a plaintiff who establishes that the fiduciary abused his or her discretion.[158]

Example 2. Former employees of the Emery Division of Quantum Chemicals Corporation, who participated in an ESOP sponsored by Quantum, brought an action against the ESOP trustees alleging that they had violated their fiduciary duties by failing to liquidate or diversify the employer stock held in the ESOP. In April 1989, Quantum sold its Emery Division to Henkel Corporation. Pursuant to this sale, Henkel agreed to continue the employment of Emery's employees and to accept from Quantum a trust-to-trust transfer of the Emery employees' benefits under Quantum's ESOP. This transfer was not completed until 18 months after the sale, by which time the value of Quantum's stock had declined from approximately $50 per share to approximately $10 per share. The court held that the ESOP trustees had not violated their fiduciary duties. The court found that

---

ciary duty arising out of a failure to diversify, or in other words, arising out of allowing the plan to become heavily weighted in company stock") (discussed in Question 34, Example 1).

158. *Moench v. Robertson*, 62 F.3d 553 (3d Cir. 1995).

the decline in the value of the Quantum stock was neither sudden and dramatic nor consistent enough to alert an objective observer at any particular time that the likely performance of the stock in the foreseeable future warranted immediate sale. Numerous investment advisors had issued reports during this time period that encouraged investors either to buy or to continue to hold Quantum stock. Moreover, both of the named plaintiffs held Quantum stock in their Section 401(k) plan accounts throughout the relevant time period, without ever attempting to liquidate or otherwise diversify these holdings. This evidence convinced the court that an adequate investigation would not have compelled a hypothetical prudent fiduciary to liquidate or diversify the Quantum stock held in the plaintiffs' ESOP accounts.[159]

Example 3. Oregon Metallurgical Corporation ("Oremet") established a stock bonus plan for its employees in the late 1980s. The

---

159. *Kuper v. Quantum Chemical Corp.*, 852 F. Supp. 1389 (S.D. Ohio 1994), *aff'd sub nom. Kuper v. Iovenko*, 66 F.3d 1447 (6th Cir. 1995). A similar fact pattern was presented in the case of *Steinman v. Hicks*, 252 F. Supp. 2d 746 (C.D. Ill.), *aff'd*, 352 F. 3d 1101 (7th Cir. 2003). The plaintiffs in the *Steinman* case were participants in a profit-sharing plan sponsored by Moorman Manufacturing Company. Moorman was acquired by the Archer-Daniels-Midland Company ("ADM") on December 30, 1997. As of that date, approximately 65% of the assets of the Moorman profit-sharing plan consisted of Moorman stock. In connection with the ADM transaction, the Moorman shares were exchanged for ADM shares. ADM then decided to terminate the Moorman plan, but it delayed distributions of the assets of the Moorman plan until a ruling as to the tax qualification of the plan could be obtained from the IRS. It took 18 months to obtain the tax ruling. By the time that the ruling was obtained and distributions of the plan assets commenced, the value of the ADM stock had declined by about one-third, from approximately $23 per share to approximately $15.56 per share. The plaintiffs argued that the trustees of the Moorman plan should have sold the ADM stock and diversified the portfolio of assets held by the plan, pending liquidation of the trust. The court rejected the plaintiffs' argument and found that the defendants had not breached their fiduciary duties by continuing to hold the ADM shares. The court noted that the plaintiffs conceded that ADM was a sound company and was a good company in which to invest, and the court found that the plaintiffs had failed to establish that a prudent fiduciary acting under similar circumstances would have made a different investment decision.

plan document stated that the plan was both a "stock bonus plan" and an ESOP that was to be invested primarily in shares of Oremet stock. A defined minimum percentage of each participant's account balance had to be invested in Oremet stock. The plan originally allowed participants to sell up to 40% of the Oremet shares allocated to their account each year. By 1996, the diversification amount was increased to 85%. In October 1997, Allegheny Teledyne and Oremet publicly announced a merger. Oremet stock closed at $23.44 per share on October 31, 1997 and at $33.88 per share on November 3, 1997, the first day of trading after the merger was announced. In January 1998, two months before the merger was closed, a group of plan participants requested the immediate release of the remaining 15% of Oremet stock in their accounts. This request was turned down. After the merger, the value of the shares of the merged enterprise decreased from $28.94 to $7.94 per share.

The plan participants who had requested that the plan be amended to permit them to sell the remaining shares of Oremet allocated to their accounts brought an action against the company and the plan fiduciaries alleging that they had breached their fiduciary responsibilities by refusing to amend the plan as requested by the plaintiffs. The court referred to the holding in the *Moench* case (described above in Example 1) and stated that a fiduciary of an eligible individual account plan who invests in employer stock is presumed to have acted consistently with ERISA, but that a plaintiff may overcome this presumption by showing that the fiduciary abused his or her discretion. The district court then went on to dismiss the plaintiffs' claim, and the court of appeals affirmed the dismissal because, unlike *Moench*, this case did not present a situation where a company's financial situation was seriously deteriorating and where there was a genuine risk of insider self-dealing.[160]

---

160. *Wright v. Oregon Metallurigical Corp.*, 360 F.3d 1090, 1097–98 (9th Cir. 2004). The court of appeals questioned the holding in *Moench* that the prudence standard continues to apply to ESOP fiduciaries with respect to the holding of employer securities and to require diversification of employer stockholdings in certain circumstances. The *Oremet* court characterized this holding as "an intermediate prudence standard" and stated that this standard was "difficult to reconcile with ERISA's statutory text, which exempts [eligible individual account

Q56 What are the primary factors for prudent diversification?

The seven factors to be considered for prudent diversification are:

1. the purposes of the plan;
2. the amount of the plan assets;
3. financial and industrial conditions;
4. the type of investment, whether mortgages, bonds, shares of stock, or otherwise;
5. distribution as to geographical location;
6. distribution as to industries; and
7. the dates of maturity.[161]

Following Plan Documents

Q57 What is required for a fiduciary to discharge his or her responsibilities in accordance with plan documents?

A fiduciary must act in accordance with the documents governing the plan to the extent that the documents are consistent with Title I of ERISA, which includes the provisions on fiduciary responsibility.[162]

---

plans] from the prudence requirement to the extent that it requires diversification." 360 F. 3d at 1097. The court of appeals in *Oremet* went on to state that interpreting the prudence requirement of ERISA to subject eligible individual account plans to an "albeit tempered duty to diversify arguably threatens to eviscerate Congressional intent and the guiding rationale behind eligible individual account plans themselves," which are exempt from the diversification requirement, because of the strong policy in favor of investments in employer stock. *Id.* Nevertheless, the court of appeals went on to state that the facts of the *Oremet* case did not necessitate that the court decide whether the *Moench* standard was appropriate because the plaintiffs' claims were unavailing even under the *Moench* standard. *See also LaLonde v. Textron, Inc.*, 270 F. Supp.2d 272, 280 (D.R.I. 2003) (applying *Moench*, and stating that "an ESOP fiduciary's presumption of reasonableness may be overcome when a precipitous decline in the employer's stock *is combined* with evidence that the company is on the brink of collapse or undergoing serious mismanagement") (*emphasis added*).

161. H.R. Conf. Rep. No. 1280, 93d Cong., 2d Sess. (1974), reprinted in U.S. Code Cong. & Ad. News 5038, at 5084-85 (1974).

162. ERISA § 404(a)(1)(D).

Q58 What is pass-through voting?

If the sponsor of an ESOP has a registration-type class of securities outstanding, then in order to be tax-qualified, the plan must grant to each participant or beneficiary power to direct the plan as to the manner in which employer securities allocated to his or her account are to be voted.[163] This is referred to as "pass-through" voting. The rights of the participants and beneficiaries to direct the voting of shares is limited to shares allocated to their accounts and does not apply to unallocated shares held in an ESOP loan suspense account. In the case of a sponsoring employer that does not have a registration-type class of securities outstanding, participants and beneficiaries must be given the right to direct the voting of shares allocated to their accounts only with respect to the approval or disapproval of the following specified matters: any corporate merger or consolidation, recapitalization, reclassification, liquidation, dissolution, sale of substantially all assets of a trade or business, or similar transactions as the Treasury Department may prescribe by regulations.[164]

> *Planning Pointer.* It should be noted that the shares of employer stock held in an ESOP trust actually are voted by the ESOP trustee. The participants and beneficiaries have the right to direct the voting of their shares but not to vote them directly. Therefore, in administering pass-through voting provisions, ESOP trustees should distribute voting instruction cards to the plan participants, not proxies. For a discussion of the procedures that an ESOP trustee should follow in soliciting voting instructions, see Questions 61 and 62.

Q59 If the plan document provides for pass-through voting, is the ESOP trustee obligated to follow voting directions that he or she receives from plan participants and beneficiaries?

Subject to two exceptions, the ESOP trustee must have the exclusive authority and discretion to manage and control the assets of the plan.[165]

---

163. Code § 409(e)(2).
164. Code § 409(e)(3).
165. ERISA § 403(a).

The two exceptions are as follows: (1) when the plan expressly provides that the trustee is subject to the direction of a named fiduciary who is not a trustee, in which case the trustee is subject to proper directions that are made in accordance with the terms of the plan and that are not contrary to ERISA; and (2) where the authority to manage, acquire, or dispose of plan assets is delegated to one or more investment managers.[166] The Department of Labor takes the position that a provision in an ESOP plan document that passes through certain decisions to the participants may satisfy the first exception to the requirement that the trustee have exclusive authority and discretion to manage and control plan assets. Therefore, if the plan document provides for pass-through voting, the trustee then must follow the directions of the participants if the directions are proper, are made in accordance with the plan terms, and are not contrary to ERISA.[167]

Q60 Can there be circumstances under which an ESOP fiduciary must disregard voting directions from plan participants and beneficiaries even though the plan document provides for pass-through voting?

Yes, in rare circumstances, the obligation of an ESOP fiduciary to comply with the terms of the plan document may be overridden by other fiduciary obligations. Section 404(c) of ERISA provides that where an individual account pension plan (such as a profit-sharing plan) permits a participant to exercise control over assets allocated to his or her account and where the participant, in fact, exercises control, the plan trustee then shall not be liable for any loss that results from the participant's exercise of control.[168] The Department of Labor regulations provide that this provision of ERISA applies only with respect to a transaction where a participant

---

166. ERISA § 403(a).
167. DOL letter to Ian D Lanoff, dated September 28, 1995, reprinted in *BNA Pension Reporter* (Oct. 9, 1995) ("Lanoff Letter").
168. This exception to the general rule that an ERISA fiduciary usually must have exclusive authority and control over plan assets does not apply to ESOPs. The Treasury Regulations provide that this provision applies only to plans that give participants a range of investments from which to choose. DOL Reg. § 2550.404c-1.

or beneficiary has exercised "independent control in fact" with respect to the investment of assets allocated to his or her individual account.[169] The regulations go on to provide that a participant does not exercise "independent control in fact" and that a direction from a participant is not valid, where the participant is subjected to improper influence by a plan fiduciary or by the plan sponsor.[170] This language suggests that an ESOP trustee may have an obligation to disregard directions that it receives from a plan participant or beneficiary with respect to the voting of employer securities where the trustee determines that the participant or beneficiary has been subjected to improper influence by another plan fiduciary or by the plan sponsor.

Q61 What procedures should an ESOP trustee follow in soliciting voting instructions?

Where participants in an ESOP have the right to direct the trustee as to how to vote the shares allocated to their accounts, the trustee should take responsibility for supervising the solicitation of voting directions from the participants. The ESOP trustee should act as an "election monitor," and its duty is to ensure free and fair pass-through voting.[171]

Q62 What specific actions should an ESOP trustee take to ensure that pass-through voting is conducted on a free and fair basis?

1. The trustee should provide a neutral explanation of the voting provisions contained in the plan document, and the trustee should provide a neutral explanation to the participants regarding how to direct the trustee as to voting shares allocated to their accounts.

2. The trustee should monitor all solicitations of voting directions from participants in the plan, so as to ensure that the participants are not subjected to improper pressure or influence from management.

---

169. DOL Reg. § 2550.404c-1(c)(1).
170. DOL Reg. § 2550.404c-1(c)(2)(i).
171. *See Shoen v. AMERCO*, 885 F. Supp. 1332 (D. Nev. 1994) (discussed above in Question 27, Example 3).

3. As a corollary to assuring that the participants are not subject to improper influence by management, the trustee should keep all participant voting instructions strictly confidential.
4. The trustee should not advise participants regarding the directions that they should provide.
5. The trustee should ensure that the participants receive sufficient accurate information to make intelligent voting decisions.
6. If the trustee is requested to forward information to the participants, he or she should review the information to ensure that it is not false or misleading.

Q63 What is "mirror voting"?

The law only requires that voting rights with respect to employer securities held by an ESOP be passed through with respect to shares that have been allocated to the accounts of participants in the plan and their beneficiaries. Unless the plan document provides otherwise, unallocated employer securities and allocated employer securities with respect to which an ESOP fiduciary receives no voting direction may be voted by the fiduciary in his or her discretion. However, many ESOP plan documents require the ESOP trustee to vote unallocated shares and allocated shares with respect to which no voting directions are received in the same proportion that the trustee votes the allocated shares with respect to which voting directions are received. This is referred to as "mirror voting."

Q64 Are ESOP trustees required to comply with mirror-voting provisions?

As stated above in Question 59, the Department of Labor takes the position that a provision in an ESOP plan document that passes voting rights through to the participants in the plan may be a valid exception to the general rule that an ESOP trustee must have exclusive authority and discretion to manage and control the plan assets. However, the Department of Labor does not extend this position to voting unallocated shares of employer stock or to voting allocated shares with respect to which no directions are provided to the ESOP trustee. With respect to these shares, the position of the Department of Labor is that, if the plan provides for mirror voting, the trustee may follow the plan provisions only to the extent permitted by Section 404(a)(1)(D) of ERISA. This provision of the law requires ESOP fiduciaries to discharge their duties "in accordance with the documents and instruments governing the plan insofar as such documents and instruments are consistent with the provisions of [Titles I and IV of ERISA]." The Department takes the position, on the one hand, that a mirror-voting provision does not diminish the extent of the trustee's duty to diligently investigate and evaluate the merits of the course of action required by the plan document to determine that the instructions are consistent with ERISA. Among other things, this means that the trustee must determine whether following the participant instructions would lead to an imprudent result. On the other hand, the DOL also takes the position that the ESOP trustee must comply with mirror-voting provisions of a plan document, "unless the trustee can articulate well-founded reasons why doing so would give rise to a violation of [Titles I and IV of ERISA]."[172] According to the DOL, the trustee may not ignore mirror-voting provisions solely because the trustee would have chosen a different course of action in the absence of those plan provisions.[173]

Q65 May an ESOP plan document grant to plan participants the authority to direct the trustee with regard to tendering of stock allocated to their accounts in response to a tender offer?

As discussed in Question 59, there is an exception to the rule that an ESOP trustee must have the exclusive authority and discretion to manage and control plan assets where the plan expressly provides that the trustee is subject to the direction of a named fiduciary who is not a trustee. In that case, the trustee is subject to proper directions that are made in accordance with the terms of the plan and that are not contrary to ERISA.[174] The exercise of any authority or control over the management or disposition

---

172. Lanoff Letter.
173. Id.
174. ERISA § 403(a)(1).

of plan assets is a fiduciary action.[175] Therefore, the decision whether to tender employer stock held by an ESOP in response to a tender offer for shares of the plan sponsor is a fiduciary act of plan management. The Department of Labor has recognized that an ESOP may grant to plan participants the authority to direct the trustee with regard to tendering of stock allocated to their own accounts and that the participants then will be considered named fiduciaries for the limited purpose of giving directions regarding the response to the tender offer. In this situation, the ESOP trustee must follow the directions of the participants if their directions are proper, are made in accordance with the plan terms, and are not contrary to ERISA.[176]

Q66 If the plan document provides that any offer to purchase shares of the plan sponsor must be passed through to the participants, must the ESOP trustee always follow the participants' directions?

Although an ESOP trustee generally must act in accordance with the plan documents, this requirement only applies to the extent that the documents are consistent with the provisions of ERISA. Therefore, the ESOP trustee must evaluate whether the participants' directions are consistent with ERISA, and if the trustee concludes that their directions are contrary to ERISA the trustee then must disregard their directions.[177]

> *Example.* A tender offer was made for all of the outstanding shares of a company that sponsored an ESOP. The ESOP trustee tendered all of the shares of the sponsoring employer that it held, without seeking direction from the participants, even though the plan provided for passing through the decision to the plan participants. The ESOP trustee concluded that the tender offer would be rejected if the decision were passed through to the plan participants because a small group of stockholders also controlled enough of the shares held by the plan to determine the tender decision if the vote were passed through. The trustee decided not to pass the decision through

---

175. ERISA § 3(21).
176. Lanoff Letter.
177. ERISA § 404(a)(D).

to the participants because rejection of the tender offer would be detrimental to the rest of the plan participants. The trustee was held to have acted properly under the circumstances.[178]

Q67 What action should an ESOP trustee take to ensure that participants' directions regarding response to a tender offer are proper?

1. The trustee should provide a neutral explanation of the provisions regarding tender offers contained in the plan, and he or she should provide a neutral explanation to the participants regarding how to direct the trustee as to tendering shares allocated to their accounts.

2. The trustee should monitor all solicitations of tender directions from participants in the plan so as to ensure that the participants are not subjected to improper pressure or influence from management.

3. As a corollary to assuring that the participants are not subject to improper influence by management, the trustee should keep all participant tender instructions strictly confidential.

4. The trustee should not advise participants regarding the directions that they should provide. (However, the trustee can provide the participants with instructions regarding how to complete and submit their direction forms to the trustee.)

5. The trustee should ensure that the participants receive sufficient accurate information to make intelligent tender decisions.

6. If the trustee is requested to forward information to the participants, he or she should review the information to ensure that it is complete and not false or misleading.

Q68 What is "mirror tendering"?

Plan documents often provide that the trustee must follow the directions of plan participants with respect to tender offers for shares of the plan sponsor's stock that has been allocated to the participants' accounts. This

---

178. *Central Trust Co. v. American Avents Corp.*, 771 F. Supp. 871 (S.D. Ohio 1989).

is sometimes referred to as "pass-through tendering." Plan documents also often require the trustee to tender unallocated shares and shares with respect to which no direction is received in the same proportion as the trustee tenders the allocated shares with respect to which instructions are received. This is referred to as "mirror tendering."

Q69 Are mirror-tendering provisions in ESOP plan documents valid?

As discussed in Question 65, the Department of Labor has recognized that an ESOP may grant to ESOP participants the authority to direct the trustee with regard to tendering of stock allocated to their own accounts and that the participants then would be considered named fiduciaries for the limited purpose of providing these instructions. In this situation, under Section 403(a)(1) of ERISA, the trustee must follow the directions of participants if those directions are proper, are made in accordance with the plan terms, and are not contrary to ERISA. However, the Department of Labor's position does not extend to unallocated shares or to allocated shares with respect to which no directions are received by the trustee. With respect to these shares, the position of the DOL is that, to the extent that the plan provisions instruct the trustee to pass through decisions regarding tender offers, the trustee may follow these provisions only to the extent permitted by Section 404(a)(1)(D) of ERISA.[179]

Section 404(a)(1)(D) of ERISA requires plan fiduciaries to discharge their duties in accordance with the plan documents insofar as they are consistent with ERISA. According to the Department of Labor, the existence of a plan provision requiring a trustee to follow participant directions in response to a tender offer "does not diminish the extent of the trustee's duty to diligently investigate and evaluate the merits of the course of action required by the plan document to determine that the instructions are consistent with [ERISA]."[180] This requires the trustee to determine whether following the participant instructions would lead to an imprudent result. However, the trustee must follow the directions that it receives from the participants unless the trustee can state well-founded reasons why doing so would result in a violation of ERISA. The trustee

---

179. Lanoff Letter.
180. *Id.* at p. 2251.

may not ignore participant instructions simply because the trustee would have chosen a different course of action if the plan did not require the trustee to follow the instructions.[181]

The only other guidance provided by the Department of Labor for ESOP trustees subject to mirror-tendering provisions is that, in the case of a tender offer, it is appropriate for the trustee to weigh the tender offer, taking into account the ability to reinvest the sale proceeds, against the likelihood that a higher value will be realized by current management and the long-term value of the company. The DOL also recommends that ESOP trustees set forth the rationale for their decision in a contemporaneous writing that can be made available to any party challenging their decision.[182]

> ***Example.*** In September 1988, Shamrock Acquisitions, III, Inc., made a tender offer for all of the outstanding common stock of Polaroid Corporation. Polaroid responded in January 1989 with a competing tender offer of its own. In addition, and partly in response to the takeover threat, Polaroid established an ESOP that acquired approximately 13.4% of Polaroid's outstanding shares. The ESOP paid $300 million for the shares, which was funded with a $15 million cash contribution from Polaroid to the plan and a $285 million loan from Polaroid to the plan. The shares purchased with cash were allocated to the accounts of the ESOP participants, and the shares purchased with the borrowed funds were allocated to a suspense account. The plan prohibited the trustee from tendering a participant's shares unless the participant specifically instructed the trustee to tender. The plan also provided that allocated shares with respect to which the trustee did not receive instructions were not to be tendered and that unallocated shares were to be tendered in the same proportion as the trustee tendered the allocated shares.
>
> The ESOP trustee, NationsBank of Georgia, N.A., mailed to all of the plan participants a brief description of the competing tender offers, advising them of their rights under the plan to instruct NationsBank either to (1) tender to Polaroid, (2) tender to Shamrock,

---

181. *Id.* at p. 2250.
182. *Id.* at p. 2251.

or (3) not tender. NationsBank informed participants that if they did not return an instruction form, this would be treated as an instruction not to tender. However, the letter from NationsBank did not inform the plan participants that unallocated shares would be tendered in the same proportion as allocated shares. NationsBank followed the plan provisions regarding the tendering of shares held by the ESOP.

The Department of Labor filed a lawsuit against NationsBank, alleging that it violated ERISA by failing to tender to Polaroid the unallocated shares and the allocated shares with respect to which no directions were provided. NationsBank argued that the participants in the ESOP were named fiduciaries with respect to the tendering of all shares held by the ESOP and that NationsBank was a directed trustee, subject only to the requirement that it follow plan provisions that are not contrary to ERISA. The court accepted this argument with respect to all of the allocated shares, including those shares for which no tender instructions were provided to NationsBank, but it rejected this argument with respect to the unallocated shares. The court held that the participants had control over the shares allocated to their accounts and that they did not lose control over these shares merely by failing to respond to a request for instructions as to how to respond to the tender offer, at least not when they were specifically told in the notice that a failure to respond would be treated as a direction not to tender.

On the other hand, the court held that the participants could not be named fiduciaries with regard to the unallocated shares. The court noted that a fiduciary must have discretion to decide the disposition of plan assets and that in order to have this discretion, a person must know that he or she can decide an issue and be aware of the available choices. The court concluded that the participants in the Polaroid ESOP were not fiduciaries with regard to the unallocated shares because they were not given notice that their action or inaction with regard to their allocated shares would control the disposition of the unallocated shares. Therefore, the court ruled that NationsBank was not a directed trustee with respect to the unallocated shares and that the applicable standard for evaluating its conduct was Section 404(a)(1)(D) of ERISA, under which NationsBank was obligated to act in the manner provided for in the plan documents insofar as they are consistent with ERISA. The court held that the mirror-tendering provisions were not inherently contrary to ERISA, but that Nations-Bank could not follow the mirror-tendering provisions blindly if the participants' directions would lead to an imprudent result. The court remanded the case for trial on the question whether NationsBank acted prudently in following the mirror-tendering provisions.[183]

---

183. *Herman v. NationsBank Trust Co.*, 126 F.3d 1354 (11th Cir. 1997).

CHAPTER 3

Prohibited Transactions

Contents

Q70	What is a prohibited transaction?	82
Q71	Are there any statutory exceptions to the prohibited-transaction provisions?	83
Q72	Are payments made to ESOP participants in satisfaction of their rights to benefits under the plan subject to the prohibited-transaction rules?	84
Q73	May a plan fiduciary receive a benefit from the plan?	85
Q74	May a person serve as a plan fiduciary if he or she is involved in a different capacity with a party in interest?	85
Q75	Who is a party in interest or a disqualified person with respect to a plan?	85
Q76	What are the differences between the prohibited-transaction rules under the Code and ERISA?	86
Q77	What plans are covered by the prohibited-transaction rules?	87
Q78	When is a fiduciary liable for engaging in a prohibited transaction under ERISA and the Code?	87
Q79	What are the penalties for engaging in a prohibited transaction?	88
Q80	Can a prohibited transaction be corrected?	89
Q81	Is the full excise tax imposed on each disqualified person who participates in a prohibited transaction?	89
Q82	May a plan purchase insurance to cover any losses to the plan resulting from a prohibited transaction?	90
Q83	What types of transactions are included in the prohibition against lending money or the extension of credit between a plan and a party in interest?	90
Q84	What is an exempt loan?	91

81

82 | Questions and Answers on the Duties of ESOP Fiduciaries

Q85 What are "qualifying employer securities"? 91

Q86 Under what circumstances are loans from a plan to participants and beneficiaries permissible? 92

Q87 May a party in interest ever furnish goods and services to a plan? 93

Q88 What is a "reasonable contract or arrangement" for furnishing goods, services, or facilities between a plan and a party in interest? 94

Q89 May a fiduciary who receives full-time pay from a sponsoring employer receive compensation for his or her services to a plan? 94

Q90 When may a fiduciary who receives full-time pay from a sponsoring employer receive reimbursement or advances for expenses incurred on behalf of the plan? 95

Q91 May plan expenses be paid out of the plan? 95

Q70 What is a prohibited transaction?

ERISA and the Internal Revenue Code (the "Code") prohibit certain transactions between plans and specified persons (called "disqualified persons" in the Code and "parties in interest" in ERISA). These transactions are referred to as "prohibited transactions." ERISA places the responsibility for prohibited transactions on the fiduciary, while the Code places the responsibility for prohibited transactions on the parties in interest who participate in the prohibited transaction.[184]

A fiduciary may not knowingly cause an employee benefit plan to engage in any of the following prohibited transactions:

1. the sale, exchange, or lease of any property between the plan and a party in interest;
2. lending money or extending credit between the plan and a party in interest;
3. furnishing goods, services, or facilities between the plan and a party in interest;
4. the transfer of plan assets to a party in interest or the use of plan assets by or for the benefit of a party in interest; or

---

184. ERISA § 406; Code § 4975(a).

5. the acquisition or holding on behalf of the plan of any "employer security" or "employer real property" in excess of the ERISA section 407 limits.[185]

In addition, a fiduciary of an employee benefit plan is prohibited from:

1. dealing with the assets of the plan in his or her own interest or for his or her own account;
2. acting in a transaction involving the plan on behalf of a party whose interests are adverse to the interests of the plan, its participants, or its beneficiaries; or
3. receiving any consideration from any party dealing with the plan in connection with a transaction involving plan assets.[186]

A transaction between a plan and a party in interest is a prohibited transaction: (1) even if the transaction normally would be considered prudent;[187] and (2) even if neither the plan nor the plan participants or beneficiaries incur a loss as a result of the transaction and the parties acted in good faith.[188]

Note. The prohibited transaction rules are intended to set forth *per se* prohibitions. Congress did not want to permit any of the listed transactions, regardless of whether they are good for the plan. Accordingly, the fact that the plan made a profit on the transaction is not a defense.

Q71 Are there any statutory exceptions to the prohibited-transaction provisions?

Yes. There are many statutory exceptions to the prohibited-transaction provisions. Some of the most important exceptions are the following:

---

185. Code § 4975(a); ERISA § 406(a).
186. Code § 4975(a); ERISA § 406(b).
187. *Leib v. Comm'r*, 88 T.C. 1474 (1987).
188. *Cutaiar v. Marshall*, 590 F.2d 523 (3d Cir. 1979).

1. loans made by a plan to a plan participant or beneficiary, if the loan satisfies certain requirements (see Question 86 for a discussion of these requirements);
2. services rendered by a party in interest to a plan that are necessary for the establishment or operation of the plan if no more than reasonable compensation is paid (see Question 87);
3. a loan to an ESOP to finance purchases of company stock, provided the interest on the loan is not in excess of a reasonable interest rate (see Question 84);
4. the acquisition or sale by a plan of qualifying employer securities, or the acquisition, sale, or lease by a plan of qualifying employer real property, under certain circumstances (see Questions 92–114); and
5. ancillary services provided by a federal or state-supervised bank or similar financial institution that is a fiduciary to the plan, under certain circumstances.[189]

If it were not for exceptions 3 and 4 above, most ESOP transactions would be impermissible. However, the exemption for purchases and sales of qualifying employer securities enables ESOPs and other individual account plans to purchase and sell employer securities, and a specific exemption for ESOPs from the prohibition on related-party loans enables ESOPs to borrow the funds necessary to finance the purchase of employer securities. For a discussion of the rules relating to purchases and sales of employer securities by ESOPs, see Questions 92–114, and for a discussion of the rules regarding ESOP loans, see Questions 83–84.

Q72 Are payments made to ESOP participants in satisfaction of their rights to benefits under the plan subject to the prohibited-transaction rules?

No. Payments of benefits to plan participants are outside the boundaries of the prohibited-transaction rules. The Supreme Court has ruled that

---

189. For a discussion of these and other statutory and administrative exemptions from the prohibited transaction rules, see S.I. Friedman et al., *ERISA Fiduciary Answer Book* (Panel Publishers 1994) ("Fiduciary Answer Book"), Questions 39–44.

payments to participants in accordance with the terms of an employee benefit plan are not "transactions" within the meaning of the ERISA prohibited-transaction rules.[190]

Q73 May a plan fiduciary receive a benefit from the plan?

Yes. Section 408(c) of ERISA provides that the prohibited-transaction rules are not to be construed as prohibiting any fiduciary from receiving any benefit to which the fiduciary may be entitled as a participant in or beneficiary of the plan, as long as the benefit is computed and paid on a basis that is consistent with the terms of the plan as applied to all other participants and beneficiaries.

Q74 May a person serve as a plan fiduciary if he or she is involved in a different capacity with a party in interest?

Yes. Section 408(c) of ERISA provides that a person may act as a fiduciary even if he or she is an officer, employee, agent, or other representative of a party in interest.

> ***Planning Pointer.*** A fiduciary who also is an officer, employee, or agent of the plan sponsor must use extra care to assure that he or she satisfies the loyalty and other fiduciary requirements when he or she acts on behalf of the plan.

Q75 Who is a party in interest or a disqualified person with respect to a plan?

A "party in interest" with respect to a plan is one of the following:

1. a fiduciary of the plan;
2. counsel to the plan;
3. an employee of the plan;
4. a person providing services to the plan;

---

190. *Lockheed Corp. v. Spink*, 517 U.S. 882, 893 (1996). *Accord, Armstrong v. Amsted Industries, Inc.*, 2004 WL 1745774 (N.D. Ill.), *rev'd on other grounds*, 446 F.3d 728 (7th Cir. 2006) (discussed in Question 29, Example 1, and Question 43).

5. an employer whose employees are covered by the plan;
6. a direct or indirect owner of 50% or more of the ownership interests in the plan sponsor;
7. an employee organization whose members are covered by the plan;
8. a relative of any of the above-described persons (with the term "relative" meaning a spouse, ancestor, lineal descendent, or spouse of a lineal descendent);
9. a corporation, partnership, trust, or estate at least 50% owned or controlled by the above-described persons;
10. an employee, officer, director, or at least 10% owner of the entities described in items 4 through 7 and 9 above; or
11. a joint venturer or partner owning at least a 10% interest in any of the entities described in items 4 through 7 and 9 above.[191]

The determination of who is a party in interest is nearly identical under ERISA and the Code. The Code, however, uses the term "disqualified person" instead of party in interest.[192]

Q76 What are the differences between the prohibited-transaction rules under the Code and ERISA?

The prohibited-transaction rules under ERISA and the Code are very similar. The main differences relate to the plans covered, the sanctions for violating the rules, and the establishment of liability for engaging in a prohibited transaction.[193] The different penalties under ERISA and the Code for violating the prohibited-transaction rules are discussed in Question 79.

---

191. ERISA, § 3(14).
192. ERISA § 3(14); Code § 4975(e)(2).
193. ERISA §§ 401 and 405; Code § 4975(e).

Q77 What plans are covered by the prohibited-transaction rules?

The prohibited-transaction rules of ERISA apply to all plans subject to ERISA—that is, in general, most pension benefit plans and most welfare benefit plans. By contrast, the prohibited-transaction rules of the Code apply only to tax-qualified plans, qualified annuities, IRAs, and individual retirement annuities. Also, the Code rules continue to apply even if the plan later loses its tax qualification.[194] Because ESOPs are tax-qualified plans, both the ERISA and the tax prohibited-transaction rules apply to them.

Q78 When is a fiduciary liable for engaging in a prohibited transaction under ERISA and the Code?

Under ERISA, a fiduciary is liable for engaging in a prohibited transaction if the fiduciary knew or should have known that he or she caused the plan to engage in a prohibited transaction. A fiduciary is liable for losses to the plan arising from a prohibited transaction in which the plan engaged if the fiduciary would have known that the transaction involving the particular party in interest was prohibited had the fiduciary acted as a prudent person. Prudence is determined based on the particular facts and circumstances of the case. In general, for a fiduciary to be prudent in the case of a significant transaction, the fiduciary must make a thorough investigation of the other party's relationship to the plan to determine whether the party is a party in interest. In the case of a normal and insubstantial day-to-day transaction, it may be sufficient to check the identity of the other party against a roster of parties in interest that is periodically updated.[195]

ERISA's knowledge requirement is not included in the Code. Therefore, a disqualified person is subject to the excise tax imposed by the IRS without proof of knowledge.[196]

---

194. ERISA Conf. Comm. Rep. at p. 5088.
195. *Id.* at 5087.
196. *Id.*

Q79 What are the penalties for engaging in a prohibited transaction?

ERISA imposes traditional trust law remedies, such as damages, and criminal penalties for a fiduciary's breach of his or her duties under ERISA.[197] See Questions 117–31 for a discussion of these remedies. The Code imposes a mandatory excise tax on a disqualified person or party in interest who participates in a prohibited transaction involving a qualified plan.[198] Although fiduciaries are disqualified persons, they are subject to the excise tax only if they act in a prohibited transaction in a capacity other than that of a fiduciary.[199]

> *Note.* The excise tax or penalty is the personal liability of the disqualified person or party in interest. The plan may not indemnify the disqualified person or party in interest for the excise taxes that he or she incurs as a result of entering into a prohibited transaction.

The excise tax is equal to 15% of the "amount involved" in the prohibited transaction for each year (or part of a year) in the "taxable period."[200] The amount involved is the greater of the fair market value of the property (and money) given or the fair market value of the property (and money) received. The valuation date for purposes of calculating the 15% excise tax is the date on which the prohibited transaction occurred.[201] The taxable period is the period beginning with the date on which the prohibited transaction occurred and ending on the earlier of (1) the date of mailing by the Secretary of the Treasury of a notice of deficiency as to the 15% tax, (2) the date the 15% tax is assessed, or (3) the date on which the "correction" of the prohibited transaction is completed.[202] A separate 15% tax is imposed for each year or part of a year in the taxable period until the correction is completed.[203] If the transaction is not corrected

---

197. ERISA §§ 501 and 502.
198. Code § 4975.
199. Code § 4975(a).
200. Code § 4975(a) and (b).
201. Code § 4975(f)(4).
202. Code § 4975(f)(2).
203. Code § 4975(a).

within the "taxable period," a tax equal to 100% of the amount involved is imposed.[204]

Q80   Can a prohibited transaction be corrected?

Yes. A prohibited transaction can be corrected by reversing the transaction to the extent possible, but in any case by placing the plan in a financial position no worse than the position it would have been in had the party in interest acted under the highest fiduciary standards.[205]

> *Note.* This requirement may be even more severe than the imposition of the excise tax (or penalty) discussed in Question 79, as the reversing of a transaction may be far costlier than the amount of tax or penalty involved. The disqualified person, however, cannot choose between paying the tax or penalty and reversing the transaction, as the tax or penalty is continuously imposed for each year the prohibited transaction remains uncorrected.

To avoid a 100% excise tax or penalty, the prohibited transaction must be corrected within the "taxable period," which is the period beginning with the date on which the prohibited transaction occurs and ending on the earliest of the following: (1) the date of the mailing of the notice of deficiency with respect to the 15% excise tax or penalty; (2) the date on which the 15% excise tax is assessed; or (3) the date on which correction of the prohibited transaction is completed.[206] The Secretary of the Treasury or of the Department of Labor may grant an extension if he or she determines that the extension is "reasonable and necessary" to correct the prohibited transaction.[207]

Q81   Is the full excise tax imposed on each disqualified person who participates in a prohibited transaction?

No. Even if more than one disqualified person participates in a prohibited transaction, only one excise tax will be imposed. However, all of the

---

204. Code § 4975(b).
205. Code § 4975(f)(5) and ERISA § 502(i).
206. Code § 4975(f)(2).
207. Treas. Reg. § 53-4963-1(e)(3).

disqualified persons participating in the prohibited transaction will be jointly and severally liable for its payment.[208]

Q82 May a plan purchase insurance to cover any losses to the plan resulting from a prohibited transaction?

Yes. A plan may carry insurance to protect itself from losses it incurs due to the misconduct of a fiduciary. A plan may not, however, contain a provision that would relieve a fiduciary of liability for a prohibited transaction.[209]

Q83 What types of transactions are included in the prohibition against lending money or the extension of credit between a plan and a party in interest?

This prohibition applies to direct and indirect loans and extensions of credit. Accordingly, a third-party loan to a plan guaranteed by a party-in-interest generally would be a prohibited transaction.[210]

> *Note.* An employer generally may not fund a plan with the employer's debt obligation because this is an indirect loan from the plan to the employer. Also, a plan may not invest in a loan made by a third party to a party in interest. Further, a plan may not acquire a debt investment under which a party in interest is the obligor.[211]

Examples of transactions found to be in violation of the prohibition against related-party loans include:

- a loan from the plan to a union that is a party in interest;[212]

---

208. Code § 4975(a) and (f)(1).
209. ERISA § 410(b).
210. ERISA § 406(a)(1)(B); Code § 4975(c)(1)(B); ERISA Conf. Comm. Rep. at p. 5088.
211. ERISA Conf. Comm. Rep. at p. 5088.
212. *Whitfield v. Tomasso*, 682 F. Supp. 1287 (E.D.N.Y. 1988).

- loans from the plan sponsor to the plan;[213] and
- loans by the plan to a corporation wholly owned by the fiduciary.[214]

Q84 What is an exempt loan?

The prohibition against the lending of money or the extension of credit between a plan and party in interest makes it generally impermissible for the sponsor of an employee benefit plan to make a loan to the plan or to guarantee a loan to the plan. However, there is a statutory exemption permitting loans to ESOPs where certain conditions are satisfied. These kinds of loans are referred to as "exempt loans." The conditions that must be satisfied in order for a loan to qualify as an exempt loan include the following:

1. the loan must be primarily for the benefit of the ESOP participants and their beneficiaries;
2. the proceeds of the loan must be used to acquire "qualifying employer securities" or to repay another exempt loan;
3. the interest rate on the loan must be reasonable;
4. the loan must be without recourse against the ESOP, and no collateral may be provided to secure the loan other than qualifying employer securities acquired with the proceeds of the loan; and
5. the loan must provide for the release from encumbrance of pledged employer securities as the loan is repaid.[215]

Q85 What are "qualifying employer securities"?

For purposes of the exempt-loan rules, the term "qualifying employer securities" generally means common stock issued by the sponsoring

---

213. *Brock v. Citizens Bank of Clovis*, 841 F.2d 344 (10th Cir 1988), *cert. denied*, 488 U.S. 829 (1988). There is an exception for interest-free loans from a plan sponsor to a plan under certain circumstances. DOL Opinion Letter 94-28A (July 21, 1994); Prohibited Transaction Exemption 80-26, 45 F.R. 28545 (April 29, 1980).
214. *Brock v. Gillikin*, 677 F. Supp. 398 (E.D.N.C. 1987).
215. Code § 4975(d)(3); Treas. Reg. § 54.4975-7(b).

employer (or by a corporation that is a member of the same controlled group) that is readily tradable on an established securities market. Where a plan sponsor has no common stock which is publicly traded, the term "qualifying employer securities" then means common stock issued by the employer (or by a corporation which is a member of the same controlled group) having a combination of voting power and dividend rights equal to or in excess of:

1. that class of common stock of the sponsoring employer (or of any corporation that is a member of the same controlled group) having the greatest voting power, and

2. that class of common stock of the sponsoring employer (or of any corporation that is a member of the same controlled group) having the greatest dividend rights.[216]

Shares of noncallable preferred stock also constitute "qualifying employer securities" if they are convertible at any time into shares of stock that meet the requirements described above and if the conversion price is reasonable.[217]

Q86 Under what circumstances are loans from a plan to participants and beneficiaries permissible?

As a result of the prohibition against the lending of money or the extension of credit between a plan and a party in interest, it generally would be impermissible for a plan to lend money to employees of the plan sponsor since employees are parties in interest to the plan. See Question 75. However, there is a statutory exemption permitting plan-loan programs if the following conditions are satisfied:

1. the loans are available to participants and beneficiaries on a reasonably equivalent basis;

---

216. Code §§ 4975(e)(8), 409(l); Treas. Reg. § 54.4975-12.
217. Code § 409(l)(3).

2. the loans are not made available to highly compensated employees in an amount greater than the amount made available to other employees;
3. the loans are made in accordance with specific provisions that are set forth in the plan;
4. the loans bear a reasonable rate of interest; and;
5. the loans are adequately secured.[218]

Q87 May a party in interest ever furnish goods and services to a plan?

Yes. A specific statutory exemption allows a plan to enter into a reasonable contract or arrangement with a party in interest (including a fiduciary) for office space, or for services that are necessary for the establishment or operation of the plan, if no more than reasonable compensation is paid.[219] As noted in Question 75, a person who provides services to a plan is a party in interest with respect to the plan. Thus, were it not for an exemption, a plan would never be permitted to receive services, even if the services are needed to run the plan properly, since any provider of services would be a party in interest.

It is important to note that although a fiduciary is also a party in interest and is subject to the exemption pertaining to the leasing of office space and the provision of services to a plan, this exemption does not always shelter a fiduciary engaging in these kinds of transactions. For example, if the fiduciary uses any of the "authority, control, or responsibility" that makes him or her a fiduciary to cause the plan to pay the fiduciary a fee for services rendered (or to pay a person in whom the fiduciary has an interest which may affect the exercise of his or her best judgment as a fiduciary), then the fiduciary has violated the fiduciary prohibitions set forth in ERISA Section 406(b).[220]

---

218. ERISA § 408(b)(1). For a more thorough discussion of the rules regarding loans by employee benefit plans, see Fiduciary Answer Book, Questions 14 through 21.
219. ERISA § 408(b)(2).
220. DOL Reg. § 2550.408b-2(e).

Planning Pointer. If a plan needs certain goods or services that a fiduciary is competent to provide, but the fiduciary cannot retain himself or herself to provide them because he or she is in a position where the exercise of his or her best judgment as a fiduciary may be compromised, the fiduciary then should withdraw from the process of selecting the individual or entity to be retained. If the plan then decides to retain the fiduciary's services, the provision of these additional services will generally not be considered a prohibited transaction.[221]

Q88 What is a "reasonable contract or arrangement" for furnishing goods, services, or facilities between a plan and a party in interest?

Although the regulations do not explain what is meant by a reasonable contract or arrangement, reasonableness is determined based on all the facts and circumstances. To come within the statutory exemption for leasing office space and the providing of services to a plan (as described in Question 87), the plan must be able to terminate the contract or arrangement on reasonably short notice without penalty. The purpose of this requirement is to prevent the plan from becoming locked into an arrangement that has become disadvantageous to it.[222]

Q89 May a fiduciary who receives full-time pay from a sponsoring employer receive compensation for his or her services to a plan?

No. However, the fiduciary may be reimbursed for "direct expenses" (see Question 90) properly and actually incurred and not otherwise reimbursed.[223]

---

221. *See* DOL Reg. § 2550.408b-2(f), Example 9.
222. DOL Reg. § 2550.408b-2(c).
223. DOL Reg. § 2550.408c-2(b)(2).

Q90 When may a fiduciary who receives full-time pay from a sponsoring employer receive reimbursement or advances for expenses incurred on behalf of the plan?

Fiduciaries may receive reimbursement of "direct expenses" properly and actually incurred on behalf of the plan and not otherwise reimbursed.[224] An expense is a direct expense if it would not have been sustained had the service not been provided and if it does not represent an allocable portion of overhead costs.[225]

A fiduciary may receive an advance to cover direct expenses that he or she will incur when performing duties for a plan if:

1. the amount of the advance is reasonable in relation to the amount of the direct expense that is likely to be incurred in the immediate future (such as during the next month); and
2. the fiduciary accounts to the plan at the end of the period covered by the advance for the expenses properly and actually incurred.[226]

Q91 May plan expenses be paid out of the plan?

Yes. Plan assets may be used to defray the reasonable expenses of administering the plan.[227] However, expenses for so-called settlor functions may not be paid out of the plan.[228] Examples of settlor functions include designing the plan, drafting the initial plan document, and terminating the plan. See the discussion of settlor functions in Question 16.

---

224. *Id.*
225. DOL Reg. § 2550.408c-2(b)(3).
226. DOL Reg. § 2550.408c-2(b)(4).
227. ERISA § 403(c)(1).
228. DOL letter to Kirk F. Maldonado, dated March 2, 1987, reprinted in *BNA Pension Reporter* (Apr. 6, 1987).

CHAPTER 4

Purchases and Sales of Employer Securities

Contents

Q92 Under what circumstances may an ESOP purchase or sell shares of the plan sponsor's stock from a party in interest? 98

Q93 What does the term "adequate consideration" mean? 99

Q94 Has the Department of Labor published regulations interpreting the term "adequate consideration"? 99

Q95 What is a "generally recognized market" for a security? 99

Q96 How do the Department of Labor regulations define the term "adequate consideration"? 101

Q97 How is the term "fair market value" defined in the adequate consideration regulations? 102

Q98 What information should be contained in the written documentation of valuation? 103

Q99 What additional information is required in the written documentation of valuation where the asset being valued is a security for which there is no generally recognized market? 104

Q100 In valuing employer securities for which there is no generally recognized market, may the existence of a "put" option be considered? 105

Q101 May an ESOP trustee pay a control premium for employer securities? 105

Q102 If an officer, director, or shareholder of the plan sponsor serves as the trustee, can the "control in fact" requirement be satisfied so as to justify the payment by the ESOP of a control premium for employer securities? 106

Q103 May an ESOP trustee pay a control premium for a minority interest combined with an option to purchase sufficient additional shares to constitute a controlling interest? 106

97

98 | Questions and Answers on the Duties of ESOP Fiduciaries

Q104 What steps should an ESOP trustee take to justify paying a control premium for a minority interest combined with a right to purchase sufficient additional shares to obtain control? 107

Q105 Are there other considerations to take into account in evaluating a "creeping control" transaction? 108

Q106 How is the "good faith" component of the adequate consideration test interpreted? 110

Q107 What must an ESOP fiduciary do to satisfy the Department of Labor that he or she has acted in good faith? 116

Q108 What are the relevant criteria for determining whether an appraiser is independent? 117

Q109 May ESOP appraisals be performed by the accountants for the plan sponsor? 119

Q110 To what extent is an ESOP trustee entitled to rely upon a valuation prepared by an independent appraiser? 119

Q111 What methods should an ESOP fiduciary employ to investigate a proposed purchase of employer securities? 124

Q112 What matters should an ESOP fiduciary direct legal counsel to investigate in connection with a proposed stock purchase? 127

Q113 Should an ESOP fiduciary become involved in contract negotiations in connection with a proposed stock purchase? 129

Q114 What additional considerations should an ESOP fiduciary take into account in a multi-investor transaction? 129

Q115 Under what circumstances may an ESOP trustee sell stock of the plan sponsor? 130

Q116 If an ESOP trustee receives an offer to purchase stock of the plan sponsor at a price in excess of the appraised value of the stock, must the stock be sold? 132

Q92 Under what circumstances may an ESOP purchase or sell shares of the plan sponsor's stock from a party in interest?

An ESOP may purchase or sell shares of the plan sponsor's stock from a party in interest if (1) the purchase or sale is for "adequate consideration," and (2) no commission is charged to the ESOP.[229]

---

229. ERISA § 408(e).

Q93 What does the term "adequate consideration" mean?

In the case of a security for which there is a generally recognized market, the term "adequate consideration" means either: (1) the price of the security prevailing on a national securities exchange that is registered under Section 6 of the Securities Exchange Act of 1934; or (2) if the security is not traded on a registered national securities exchange, then the term "adequate consideration" means a price not less favorable to the plan than the offering price for the security as established by the current bid and asked prices quoted by persons independent of the issuer and of any party in interest.[230]

In the case of an asset other than a security for which there is a generally recognized market, the term "adequate consideration" means the fair market value of the asset as determined in good faith by the trustee or named fiduciary pursuant to the terms of the plan and in accordance with regulations published by the Secretary of Labor.[231]

Q94 Has the Department of Labor published regulations interpreting the term "adequate consideration"?

The Department of Labor published proposed regulations under Section 3(18)(B) of ERISA in 1988.[232] After 20 years, these proposed regulations still have not been issued in final form. Although the regulations interpreting Section 3(18)(B) of ERISA (the "adequate consideration regulations") continue in form to be only proposed regulations, most ESOP consultants believe that they provide important guidance for ESOP trustees and other fiduciaries in evaluating proposed purchases and sales of employer securities.

Q95 What is a "generally recognized market" for a security?

The adequate consideration regulations do not define this term and do not analyze the requirements of Section 3(18)(A) of ERISA. In the preamble to the adequate consideration regulations, the Department of Labor stated that the question whether a security is one for which there

---

230. ERISA § 3(18)(A).
231. ERISA § 3(18)(B).
232. Prop. DOL Reg. § 2510.3-18.

is a generally recognized market "requires a factual determination in light of the character of the security and the nature and extent of market activity with regard to the security."[233] Generally, the Department of Labor will examine whether a security is being actively traded so as to provide the benchmarks Congress intended. Isolated trading activity, or trades between related parties, generally will not be considered by the Department of Labor to be sufficient to show the existence of a generally recognized market for a security.[234] There are no cases or rulings interpreting the term "generally recognized market," as that term is used in ERISA, but the IRS has issued rulings interpreting a similar term for federal income tax purposes.

> *Example 1.* A, B, and C planned to sell their shares to an ESOP. They desired to elect to defer tax upon the gain that they would realize in connection with the sale under the provisions of Section 1042 of the Code. An election pursuant to Code Section 1042 can only be made with respect to stock issued by a domestic corporation that has no stock outstanding "that is readily tradable on an established securities market."[235] The shares held by A, B, and C constituted approximately 58% of the outstanding shares of the corporation, and their shares were subject to SEC rules concerning private placements. There was very little trading in the company's stock. Approximately 2,100 of the corporation's 270,000 outstanding shares were sold in the prior year. An individual was able to purchase 100 shares only after several months of searching on a public stock exchange. The company's common stock was not listed on any exchange registered under Section 6 of the Securities Exchange Act of 1934 and was not quoted on a system sponsored by a national securities association registered under Section 15A(b) of the Securities Exchange Act. The IRS ruled that the shares proposed to be sold by A, B, and C to the ESOP were not readily traded on an established securities market and, therefore, constituted "qualified securities" for purposes of Section 1042 of the Code.[236]

---

233. Prop. DOL Reg. § 2510.3-18, preamble, §A.
234. Id.
235. Code § 1042(c)(1).
236. Priv. Ltr. Rul. 8727025 (Apr. 12, 1987).

Example 2. The shares of Company M were deregistered on July 16, 1989, and the stock ceased to be listed on NASDAQ on that date. Thereafter the stock was listed on the "pink sheets," which reflected the names of two market makers. Shareholders A and B of Company M requested a ruling from the IRS that: (1) upon the termination of the quotation of Company M common stock on the NASDAQ system on July 16, 1989, the shares would not be "readily tradable on an established securities market;" and (2) the shares of Company M held by shareholders A and B constituted "qualified securities" within the meaning of Section 1042(c)(1) of the Code. The IRS ruled that Company M's common stock ceased to be "readily tradable on an established market" when the shares ceased to be traded on NASDAQ. However, the IRS also held that the shares held by A and B were not "qualified securities" within the meaning of Section 1042(c)(1) of the Code because the shares had not been issued by a domestic corporation that had no stock outstanding that was readily tradable on an established securities market for at least one year before and immediately after the sale, as required by Section 1.1042-1T of the Temporary Income Tax Regulations.[237]

Planning Pointer. ESOP trustees should require that current independent appraisals be provided as the basis for determining the price at which employer securities will be purchased or sold unless the employer securities are actively traded on an established exchange. By relying upon a current independent appraisal, the ESOP trustee can protect against being second-guessed as to whether there is a generally recognized market for the employer securities.

Q96 How do the Department of Labor regulations define the term "adequate consideration"?

The adequate consideration regulations establish a two-part test for determining "adequate consideration." First, the purchase or sale price must reflect the security's fair market value and, second, this value must result from a determination made by the plan trustee or named

---

237. Priv. Ltr. Rul. 9036039 (Jun. 13, 1990).

fiduciary in good faith.[238] The preamble to the adequate consideration regulations make clear that both the fair market value and the good-faith requirements must be satisfied in order for the adequate consideration exemption to apply.

Q97 How is the term "fair market value" defined in the adequate consideration regulations?

The term "fair market value" is defined as the price at which an asset would change hands between a willing buyer and a willing seller when the former is not under any compulsion to buy and the latter is not under any compulsion to sell, and both parties are able, as well as willing, to trade and are well-informed about the asset and the market for the asset.[239] In addition to this general formulation of the definition of fair market value, the adequate consideration regulations set forth two additional specific

---

238. Prop. DOL Reg. § 2510.3-18(b)(1)(ii). Most courts have embraced the two-part test for determining whether the "adequate consideration" requirement has been satisfied. *See, e.g., Keach v. U.S. Trust Co., N.A.*, 419 F.3d 626 (7th Cir. 2005) (discussed in Question 106, Example 4); *Chao v. Hall Holding Co.*, 285 F.3d 415, 436 (6th Cir. 2002) (discussed in Question 110, Example 3); *Eyler v. Comm.*, 88 F.3d 445, 454–55 (7th Cir. 1996) (discussed in Question 106, Example 2); *In re: Unisys Savings Plan Litigation*, 74 F.3d 420, 434 (3d Cir. 1996); *Katsaros v. Cody*, 744 F.2d 270, 279 (2d Cir. 1984); *Donovan v. Cunningham*, 716 F.2d 1455, 1467 (5th Cir. 1983) (discussed in Question 106, Example 1); and *Donovan v. Mazzola*, 716 F.2d 1226, 1231 (9th Cir. 1983). See also *Henry v. Champlain Enterprises, Inc.*, 334 F. Supp. 2d 252, 269–70 (N.D.N.Y. 2004) rev'd, 445 F.3d 610 (2d Cir. 2006); *Horn v. McQueen*, 215 F. Supp. 2d 867, 875 (W.D. Ky. 2002) (discussed in Question 106, Example 3); and *Reich v. Valley Nat'l. Bank of Arizona*, 837 F. Supp. 1259, 1280 (S.D.N.Y. 1993) (the two-part test is "unitary and conjunctive") (discussed in Question 49, Example 2, and in Question 51). However, the Eighth Circuit has allowed the adequate consideration exception to be invoked where only one element of the two-part test set forth in the regulations is proven by the fiduciary. *Herman v. Mercantile Bank, N.A.*, 143 F.3d 419 (8th Cir. 1998). There, the court stated that "[e]ven if the trustee fails to make a good faith effort to determine the fair market value of the stock, '[it] is insulated from liability if a hypothetical prudent fiduciary would have made the same decision anyway.'" *Id.* at 421 (quoting from *Roth v. Sawyer-Cleator Lumber Co.*, 16 F.3d 915, 919 [8th Cir. 1994]).

239. Prop. DOL Reg. § 2510.3-18(b)(2)(i).

requirements. First, fair market value must be determined as of the date of the transaction involving the asset being valued and, second, the fair market value of the asset must be reflected in written documentation satisfying specified conditions.[240]

Q98 What information should be contained in the written documentation of valuation?

The adequate consideration regulations require the written documentation of valuation to contain the following information:

- a summary of the qualifications of the person making the valuation to evaluate assets of the type being valued;
- a statement of the asset's value, a statement of the methods used in determining that value, and the reasons for the valuation in light of those methods;
- a full description of the asset being valued;
- the factors taken into account in making the valuation, including any restrictions, understandings, agreements, or obligations limiting the use or disposition of the property;
- the purpose for which the valuation was made;
- the relevance or significance accorded to the valuation methodologies taken into account;
- the effective date of the valuation; and
- in cases where a valuation report has been prepared, the signature of the person making the valuation and the date the report was signed.[241]

---

240. Prop. DOL Reg. § 2510.3-18(b)(2)(ii), (iii).
241. Prop. DOL Reg. § 2510.3-18(b)(4)(i). Additional information is required where the asset being valued is a security other than a security for which there is a generally recognized market. See Question 99.

Q99 What additional information is required in the written documentation of valuation where the asset being valued is a security for which there is no generally recognized market?

Where the asset being valued for the purpose of establishing an exemption from the general prohibition upon related-party purchases and sales of assets is a security for which there is no generally recognized market, the written documentation of valuation must contain, in addition to the information described in Question 98, an assessment of the following factors:

- the nature of the business and the history of the enterprise from its inception;
- the economic outlook in general, and the condition and outlook of the specific industry in particular;
- the book value of the securities and the financial condition of the business;
- the earning capacity of the company;
- the dividend-paying capacity of the company;
- whether or not the enterprise has goodwill or other intangible value;
- the market price of securities of corporations engaged in the same or a similar line of business which are actively traded in a free and open market, either on an exchange or over the counter;
- the marketability of the securities; and
- whether or not the seller would be able to obtain a control premium from an unrelated third party with regard to the block of securities being valued.[242]

---

242. Prop. DOL Reg. § 2510.3-18(b)(4)(ii).

Q100 In valuing employer securities for which there is no generally recognized market, may the existence of a "put" option be considered?

The Department of Labor takes the position that the existence of a "put" option should be considered for valuation purposes only to the extent that the option is enforceable and that the employer has, and may reasonably be expected to continue to have, adequate resources to meet its obligations. Thus, the Department of Labor requires ESOP fiduciaries to assess whether these "put" rights actually are enforceable and whether the employer will be able to pay for the securities when and if they are exercised, taking into account the company's financial strength and liquidity.[243] While the existence of the put option *may* preclude the need for a marketability discount, courts will examine the terms of the put option to determine whether a marketability discount is appropriate in any particular case.[244]

Q101 May an ESOP trustee pay a control premium for employer securities?

The Department of Labor takes the position that an ESOP trustee may pay a control premium for employer securities only to the extent that an unrelated third party would pay a control premium.[245] Where a control premium is taken into account, the proposed regulations require (1) that actual control (both in form and in substance) be passed to the ESOP with the sale, or will be passed to the ESOP within a reasonable time pursuant to a binding agreement in effect at the time of the sale, and (2) that it must be reasonable to assume that the ESOP's control will not be dissipated within a short period of time after the purchase.[246]

The Department of Labor has stated that it will carefully scrutinize transactions where ESOPs pay a control premium to acquire employer

---

243. Prop. DOL Reg. § 2510.3-18(b)(4)(ii)(H).
244. See *Eyler v. Comm'r.*, 69 T.C.M. 2200, *aff'd*, 88 F.3d 445 (7th Cir. 1996) (discussed in Question 106, Example 2). See also *Reich v. Valley Nat'l. Bank*, 837 F. Supp. 1259, 1283-1284 (S.D.N.Y. 1993) (discussed in Question 49, Example 2, and Question 51).
245. Prop. DOL Reg. § 2510.3-18 (preamble, § B5).
246. Prop. DOL Reg. § 2510.3-18(b)(4)(ii)(I).

securities, so as to determine whether the transaction actually results in the passing of control to the plan. For example, the Department of Labor has stated that it may be difficult to determine that a plan paying a control premium has received control in fact where it is reasonable to assume, at the time of the purchase of the employer securities, that distribution of shares to plan participants will cause the plan's control of the plan sponsor to be dissipated within a short period of time after the purchase.[247]

Q102 If an officer, director, or shareholder of the plan sponsor serves as the trustee, can the "control in fact" requirement be satisfied so as to justify the payment by the ESOP of a control premium for employer securities?

The Department of Labor has stated that an ESOP will not be deemed to have failed to have obtained control merely because individuals who previously were officers, directors, or shareholders of the plan sponsor continue as plan fiduciaries or corporate officers after the ESOP acquires the employer securities. However, the Department of Labor also has noted that the retention of management and the use of corporate officers as plan fiduciaries, when viewed in conjunction with other facts, may indicate that actual control has *not* passed to the ESOP.[248]

Q103 May an ESOP trustee pay a control premium for a minority interest combined with an option to purchase sufficient additional shares to constitute a controlling interest?

The proposed Department of Labor regulations provide that an ESOP trustee may pay a control premium for employer securities either where the ESOP obtains actual control with the purchase or where actual control will be passed to the ESOP "within a reasonable time pursuant to a binding agreement in effect at the time of the sale."[249]

---

247. Prop. DOL Reg. § 2510.3-18(b)(4)(ii)(I) (preamble, § B5).
248. *Id.*
249. Prop. DOL Reg. § 2510.3-18(b)(4)(ii)(I)(1).

Q104 What steps should an ESOP trustee take to justify paying a control premium for a minority interest combined with a right to purchase sufficient additional shares to obtain control?

Other than the vague and general guidelines described above in Question 103, no guidance for ESOP trustees in this situation is provided by ERISA or by the final or proposed Department of Labor regulations. Moreover, no guidance is provided by the case law. Experienced ESOP lawyers generally recommend that ESOP trustees take the following steps to justify paying a control premium in a "creeping control" transaction:

1. The option for the ESOP trustee to obtain a controlling interest should be arranged as part of the initial sale transaction, and the ESOP trustee should not pay any additional consideration for the option.

2. The ESOP trustee should have the right to exercise the option either in whole or in part.

3. The ESOP trustee should be able to exercise the option within a reasonable period of time after the initial purchase. What constitutes a "reasonable" period of time should be based on the facts and circumstances, including, in particular, the ability of the sponsoring employer to finance the transaction. For example, if the term of the original ESOP loan is five years, a second purchase arguably would occur "within a reasonable period of time" after the first purchase if it is timed to coincide with repayment in full of the original loan.[250]

4. The sponsoring employer and, perhaps, the selling shareholders should commit to guarantee or otherwise facilitate financing for the

---

250. The Department of Labor has challenged a number of "two-step" or "multi-step" transactions under which ESOPs have paid a control price for a minority interest in a corporation together with a long-term option to acquire sufficient additional shares to bring the ESOP's ownership interest above 50%. The Department of Labor has taken the position in these cases that the ESOP must obtain a controlling interest within two years of the original transaction. The proceedings that the Department of Labor has undertaken in cases involving "creeping control" transactions all have been resolved at the administrative level, and no courts have ruled on the position taken by the Department of Labor.

exercise by the ESOP trustee of the option. Unless access to financing is provided for the ESOP trustee, the Department of Labor or a court may find the option granted to the ESOP to be lacking in substance.

5. Consideration should be given to the grant of a proxy to the ESOP trustee covering enough shares to give it voting control immediately after the initial purchase. Of course, this provides the ESOP with actual control, and for the Department of Labor or the courts to require this would substantially negate the recognition in the adequate consideration regulations that a control premium may be paid where control will be obtained within a reasonable time.

6. The ESOP trustee should obtain "go-along" rights, pursuant to which a controlling shareholder will be allowed to sell to a third party only if the buyer agrees to also purchase the shares held by the ESOP at the same price and on the same terms as offered to the controlling shareholders.

7. The ESOP trustee should obtain protection against dilution of its right to obtain a controlling interest by means of limitations on future share issuances by the sponsoring employer.

8. The plan document should provide that when a participant is entitled to receive benefits, the shares of the sponsoring employer allocated to his or her account will be valued on a controlling-interest basis. This will assure that the shares of the plan participants are valued on the same basis as the shares sold by the selling shareholder.

Often, it will not be possible for an ESOP trustee to obtain all of the protections described above. Where some but not all of these protections can be obtained, the question whether it is appropriate for the ESOP trustee to pay a control premium will depend on the facts and circumstances surrounding the particular transaction.

Q105 Are there other considerations to take into account in evaluating a "creeping control" transaction?

Yes. In addition to the valuation and control issues described above in Questions 101–4, where it is proposed that an ESOP will acquire an option or other right to purchase additional employer securities, consideration should be given to whether the option or right is an appropriate investment for an ESOP. ESOPs and other employee benefit plans may invest only in "qualifying employer securities."[251] A plan fiduciary is prohibited from acquiring, on behalf of the plan, any employer security that is not a qualifying employer security.[252] The term "employer security" is defined to mean a security issued by the plan sponsor or by an affiliate of the plan sponsor.[253] By analogy to the definition of the term "security" for securities law purposes, an option or right to purchase securities should itself be deemed to be a security. However, an option or purchase right granted to an ESOP by a selling shareholder may not constitute an "employer security" because the option or right is not granted by the sponsoring employer. It might be argued that the option or right to purchase is an "employer security" because the selling shareholder is an "affiliate" of the sponsoring employer, but it is not clear whether this argument would be accepted by the Department of Labor or by a court. Moreover, even if the option or right to purchase qualifies as an "employer security," it nevertheless may not be a "qualifying employer security." The term "qualifying employer security" is defined to mean an employer security that is (1) stock, (2) a marketable obligation, or (3) an interest in a publicly traded partnership.[254] Since an option or purchase right is not stock, an option or purchase right may not be a "qualifying employer security." However, there are no reported cases in which the Department of Labor has taken this position.

> ***Planning Pointer.*** To avoid this possible problem, the selling shareholder seeking a control price for his or her shares could grant to the sponsoring employer an option to purchase his or her shares, and this option or right could be assignable to the ESOP. The ESOP could obtain a controlling interest if either: (1) the sponsoring employer purchases sufficient additional shares so as to increase the ESOP's percentage ownership to greater than 50%; or (2) the option or pur-

---

251. ERISA § 407(a)(1)(A).
252. ERISA § 406(a)(1)(E).
253. ERISA § 407(d)(1).
254. ERISA § 407(d)(5).

chase right is assigned upon exercise to the ESOP. In this situation, arguably the only "securities" are held by the sponsoring employer and the selling shareholder.

Q106 How is the "good faith" component of the adequate consideration test interpreted?

As stated above in Question 96, the adequate consideration regulations establish a two-part test for determining adequate consideration in an ESOP transaction. First, the price for the employer securities to be purchased or sold must reflect their fair market value and, second, fair market value must be determined by the ESOP trustee or named fiduciary in good faith.[255] The adequate consideration regulations state that the requirement that the fiduciary determine fair market value in good faith establishes an objective, rather than a subjective, standard of conduct and that an assessment of whether a fiduciary has acted in good faith will be made in light of all relevant facts and circumstances.[256]

The first court to interpret the adequate consideration provisions of Section 3(18) of ERISA defined its task, in reviewing the price paid by an ESOP for shares of the plan sponsor, to be to ask whether the price paid for the shares was "the fair market value of the asset as determined in good faith by the . . . fiduciary."[257] The court stated that its task was *not* to redetermine the appropriate amount for itself *de novo*, but the court rejected the ESOP fiduciaries' contention that their subjective good faith in setting a purchase price was all that the law required. Rather, the court concluded that the statutory reference to "good faith" in Section 3(18) of ERISA must be read in light of the overriding fiduciary duties set forth in Section 404 of ERISA. Doing this, the court held that the ESOP fiduciaries could satisfy their burden to prove that adequate consideration was paid by showing that they arrived at their determination of fair market value by way of a prudent investigation under the circumstances then prevailing. The court stated that its task was not a search for subjective good faith and went on to make one of the most famous statements in

---

255. Prop. DOL Reg. § 2510.3-18(b)(1)(ii).
256. Prop. DOL Reg. § 2510.3-18(b)(3)(i).
257. *Donovan v. Cunningham*, 716 F.2d 1455, 1467 (5th Cir. 1983), *cert. denied*, 467 U.S. 1251 (1984).

all of employee benefits case law: "a pure heart and an empty head are not enough."[258]

Example 1. Kenneth R. Cunningham was the chairman of the board, chief executive officer, and sole shareholder of Metropolitan Contract Services, Inc. ("MCS"), during 1975 and 1976. In those years, he sold shares of MCS to the MCS ESOP in two separate transactions, one in August 1976 and the second in February 1977. The Secretary of Labor brought an action against five ESOP fiduciaries, including Mr. Cunningham, alleging that they had breached their fiduciary duties and engaged in prohibited transactions by causing the ESOP to purchase the shares from Mr. Cunningham at prices in excess of fair market value. The fiduciaries all were officers and directors of MCS. In determining the value of the MCS stock, the fiduciaries relied upon the appraisal of an independent investment banking firm, which was dated as of June 30, 1975. The parties stipulated that the appraisal was accurate as of its date. The crucial question identified by the court was whether the fiduciaries prudently determined that the appraisal remained accurate at the time of the two ESOP transactions, 13 and 20 months later. The court concluded that the reliance by the ESOP fiduciaries on the appraisal report was imprudent because, among other things, the revenues of MCS for the years 1976 and 1977 were consistently and significantly below those anticipated by the appraisal report, and this should have alerted the fiduciaries that the appraisal was seriously out of date.[259]

Example 2. In early 1986, Gary L. Eyler, the controlling shareholder of Continental Training Services, Inc. ("CTS"), decided to take CTS public through an initial public offering. Two independent investment banking firms were retained as underwriters. In September 1986, a preliminary prospectus was filed on behalf of CTS with the Securities and Exchange Commission. The underwriters determined

---

258. *Id.* at 1467. Accord, *Eyler v. Comm'r*, 88 F.3d 445 (7th Cir. 1996) (discussed in Question 106, Example 2); *Reich v. Hall Holding Co.*, 21 EBC (BNA) 2429 (N.D. Ohio 1998) (discussed in Question 110, Example 3).

259. *Donovan v. Cunningham*, 716 F.2d 1455 (5th Cir. 1983), *cert. denied*, 467 U.S. 1251 (1984).

an estimated range of the offering price for CTS stock between $13 and $16 per share. The underwriters attempted to sell the shares of CTS during October and early November 1986, but found little interest in the CTS stock in the $13–$16 price range. The offering was cancelled, and in December 1986 CTS formed an ESOP. On December 22, 1986, Eyler sold to the ESOP 689,655 of his shares of CTS stock (representing approximately 13.7% of the total outstanding shares of CTS) for a price of $14.50 per share, or approximately $10 million. Meanwhile, earlier in 1986, two investigations of CTS had been commenced, one by the State of California and one by the U.S. Department of Education. The IRS asserted that the price paid by the ESOP for Eyler's shares exceeded their fair market value and that the sale by Eyler of his shares to the ESOP was therefore a prohibited transaction. The IRS assessed $12.5 million in excise taxes against Eyler—$500,000 per year for the years 1986–1990 (when the first-tier excise tax was equal to 5% of the amount involved), and an additional $10 million for the year 1990, by reason of Eyler's failure to correct the prohibited transaction within the correction period.

Eyler sought a refund of the excise taxes. The court stated that Eyler would prevail if he could prove either (1) that the fair market value of the stock of CTS that he sold to the ESOP was at least $14.50 per share, or (2) that the $14.50 price was determined in good faith by way of a prudent investigation. With respect to the value of the stock, Eyler argued that the $14.50-per-share price was supported by the estimated offering price range for the stock determined by the underwriters. The court rejected Eyler's argument, on the grounds that the underwriters had not purported to determine the fair market value of CTS as of a specific point in time and that the estimated offering price range was based on the following assumptions that were not present at the time of the ESOP transaction: (1) a public marketplace for the stock of CTS; (2) a successful initial public offering, resulting in a significant capital infusion to CTS; and (3) the absence of an ESOP with its attendant debt and minimum-contribution requirements.

With respect to the question whether the ESOP fiduciaries had acted in good faith in determining the price to be paid by Eyler's stock, the court found that the fiduciaries could not properly rely upon the estimated price range for the stock determined by the underwriters because the attempted public offering had failed. In addition, the fiduciaries knew that CTS was under investigation by the State of California and by the U.S. Department of Labor and that CTS would have to guarantee a $10 million loan in connection with the ESOP transaction. The court concluded that, with knowledge of these facts, the ESOP fiduciaries' duties to investigate was not satisfied by reliance upon the letter they had obtained from the underwriters. Therefore, the court upheld the imposition of the excise tax.[260]

Example 3. In December 1993, Milton Thompson and Robert McQueen were appointed to serve as the trustees of a newly created ESOP sponsored by U.S. Corrections Corporation ("USCC"). Thompson and McQueen both were stockholders in and officers of USCC. The ESOP was established for the purpose of acquiring the shares of USCC held by a third shareholder, Richard Todd, who desired to retire. Thompson and McQueen wanted to maintain control of the company, and they consulted with a banker and an accountant regarding ways to buy out Todd. The consultants suggested the use of an ESOP.

The trustees entered into a stock purchase agreement with Todd without negotiating the price, without the benefit of any valuation work, and at the price suggested by the accountant in connection with his informal structuring proposals. The trustees then hired the accountant to perform the appraisal. The trustees also failed to retain independent legal counsel. The court held that the trustees had violated the requirements of Section 406 of ERISA by failing to conduct an independent and prudent investigation of the ESOP stock purchase. The court found that the trustees had not reviewed the transaction from the perspective of acquiring the stock at the lowest price possible and that, to the extent that they were involved in any investigation as to the value of the stock at all, they were not investigating or acting on behalf of the ESOP. In support of its holding, the court noted, among other things: (1) that the price paid by the ESOP for the shares was not reached through negotiations between the trustees and the selling shareholder; (2) that the ESOP trustees

---

260. *Eyler v. Comm'r.*, 69 T.C.M. 2200 (1995), *aff'd*, 88 F.3d 445 (7th Cir. 1996).

were not independent and that they failed to obtain advice from any independent legal or financial advisors; and (3) that the entire transaction was arranged and closed in a compressed time frame, due to a closing deadline imposed by the selling shareholders.[261]

The cases described in the above three examples all illustrate imprudent behavior by ESOP trustees. Example 4 describes a case where an experienced ESOP trustee was held by a court to have satisfied its fiduciary responsibilities notwithstanding that the plan sponsor went bankrupt within six years of a large purchase of employer stock by the ESOP trustee.

Example 4. In December 1995, an ESOP sponsored by Foster & Gallagher, Inc. ("F&G"), purchased shares of F&G from several F&G officers and directors for a price of approximately $70 million. F&G was a direct-mail marketing company engaged in the marketing of horticultural and other products through the mail. It employed various direct-mail sweepstakes promotions to its customers. For the first two years following the ESOP transaction, F&G remained very profitable. During this period, the attorneys general of two states began investigations of F&G's sweepstakes practices. Both of these investigations were settled in the summer of 1998 through the payment of $70,500 in costs and certain injunctive relief. By 1998, F&G stopped employing one of the three primary sweepstakes marketing formats it had traditionally used. In February 1998, several news stories appeared focusing on the sweepstakes practices of American Family Publishing and Publishers Clearing House. Although F&G did not use many of the practices that were criticized in those news reports, the negative publicity about sweepstakes in general caused an immediate and dramatic decline in F&G's consumer-response rates. The negative publicity resulted in class actions and multi-state governmental enforcement actions against other direct-mail marketers, which further fed the anti-sweepstakes sentiment. F&G's profits began to decline steadily in 1998, and F&G was forced to declare bankruptcy in 2001. Participants in the F&G ESOP brought an ac-

---

261. *Horn v. McQueen*, 215 F. Supp. 2d 867 (W.D. Ky. 2002).

tion against the ESOP trustee, U.S. Trust Company, and officers and directors of F&G alleging violations of ERISA in connection with the 1995 ESOP stock purchase. The gist of the plaintiffs' complaint was that U.S. Trust had breached its fiduciary duty by failing to adequately assess the risks associated with F&G's use of sweepstakes promotions in determining the purchase price to pay for the F&G stock.

The district court found that U.S. Trust had gone to considerable lengths to understand F&G's business and to assess independently the merits of the transaction, including interviewing members of management, visiting F&G's facilities, reviewing the company's business plans, and examining financial documents. The district court also noted that U.S. Trust had engaged in active negotiations regarding the purchase price and that, as a result, the price had been reduced by almost 20% from the original price offered by the selling shareholders. With respect to F&G's marketing practices, the court found that neither its dependency on sweepstakes nor the increase in governmental regulation of the sweepstakes industry posed a material risk to F&G in 1995 or a foreseeable material risk in the future. Therefore, the district court held that U.S. Trust had conducted a sufficient investigation into the merits of the ESOP transaction. In the alternative, the district court determined that, even if U.S. Trust had breached a fiduciary duty, it was not liable for damages because the losses to the ESOP were not caused by the alleged breach. The court found that the cause of the loss to the ESOP was the collapse in customer response rates that started in 1998 after the wave of negative publicity surrounding the American Family Publishers scandal. Accordingly, the loss to the ESOP was not due to any meaningful risk from F&G's dependency on sweepstakes promotions in 1995 or from governmental regulation of sweepstakes at that time.[262]

On appeal, the plaintiffs argued that a prudent investor would have wanted to know whether state regulation of F&G's sweepstakes promotions could have a material effect on the finances of F&G. Therefore, the plaintiffs argued that U.S. Trust should have taken a careful look at the sweepstakes issues, which were not identified in the due diligence review undertaken by U.S. Trust and its financial

---

262. *Keach v. U.S. Trust Co., N.A.*, 313 F. Supp. 2d 818 (C.D. Ill. 2004).

and legal advisors. The court of appeals was troubled by the absence in the record of any communications between U.S. Trust and its lawyers regarding the sweepstakes issues. However, the court concluded that the fact that the due diligence review failed to identify any sweepstakes issues did not negate the reasonableness of the overall analysis of the merits of the ESOP transaction conducted by U.S. Trust under the circumstances prevailing in 1995. The court of appeals found that the record established that the overlooked matter was one that no one perceived to be a material concern at the time or to be outcome-determinative; hence, it could not be said that the overall investigation was imprudent. Therefore, the court of appeals affirmed the holding of the district court.[263]

Q107 What must an ESOP fiduciary do to satisfy the Department of Labor that he or she has acted in good faith?

The Department of Labor interprets the good-faith requirement to mean that:

1. The fiduciary must have arrived at a determination of fair market value through a prudent investigation of the circumstances existing at the time of the valuation and the application of sound business valuation principles; and

2. The fiduciary making the valuation either (1) must be independent of all parties to the transaction, or (2) must rely on the report of an appraiser who is independent of all parties to the transaction.[264]

For a discussion of the specific methods that an ESOP fiduciary should employ to investigate a proposed purchase of employer securities, see Question 111.

---

263. *Keach v. U.S. Trust Co., N.A.*, 419 F.3d 626 (7th Cir. 2005) (also discussed in Question 111).
264. Prop. DOL Reg. § 2510.3-18(b)(3)(ii).

Example. In the *Foster & Gallagher* case described in Question 106, Example 4, the court held that the ESOP trustee had fulfilled its fiduciary responsibilities in connection with a $70 million purchase of employer stock, notwithstanding the fact that the plan sponsor went bankrupt less than six years after the stock purchase. The court based its ruling on the careful review of the investigation undertaken by the trustee before the stock purchase. As discussed in the example in Question 106, the court was impressed with the financial analysis and the financial due-diligence investigation undertaken by the trustee and by its financial advisor.[265]

Q108 What are the relevant criteria for determining whether an appraiser is independent?

The adequate consideration regulations state that, in order to satisfy the independence requirement, an appraiser must in fact be independent of all parties participating in the transaction. Among other things, this means that the appraiser (1) should not be controlled by, or under common control with, any of the parties to the transaction, (2) should not be an officer, director, employee, employer, or relative of any parties to the transaction, and (3) should not be a corporation or partnership of which any party to the transaction is an officer, director, or partner.[266] In addition, the appraiser should be selected by the plan fiduciary, and the plan fiduciary should have the right to terminate the appraiser's appointment. In the absence of these circumstances, the appraiser may be unable to be completely neutral in performing the appraisal.[267] However, the Department of Labor has recognized that the independence of an appraiser will not be affected solely by reason of the fact that his or her fee is paid by the plan sponsor.

Example. In 1992, the ESOP committee under the Aetna Plywood, Inc., Employee Stock Ownership Plan agreed to sell the shares of Aetna Plywood stock held by the plan. At that time, the ESOP owned

---

265. *Keach v. U.S. Trust Co., N.A.*, 313 F. Supp. 2d 818, 868 (C.D. Ill. 2004), *aff'd*, 419 F.3d 626 (7th Cir. 2005).
266. Prop. DOL Reg. § 2510.3-18(b)(3)(iii).
267. Prop. DOL Reg. § 2510.3-18 (preamble, § B3).

all of the outstanding shares of the company, except for 17 shares held by the president of the company, Jeffrey G. Davis. As a result of the transaction, Davis became the sole shareholder of the company. The members of the ESOP committee were Davis, the chief financial officer of the company, and two friends of Mr. Davis who had no relationship with the company. The price at which the shares were sold by the ESOP was determined by Ollie Turner, a business appraiser who had been preparing the annual valuations of the company's stock for many years and who also had provided advice to Davis and to Davis's father regarding business planning matters. In order to confirm Turner's valuation, Aetna obtained a valuation opinion from Walter Zweifler, another business appraiser, and a fairness opinion from Edward Cerar, of Corporate Valuation Specialists, Inc. Zweifler and Cerar were recommended by Turner.

A former employee of the company brought a class action against the ESOP fiduciaries, alleging that they agreed to sell the company stock held by the ESOP at a price below fair market value pursuant to a plan to enable Davis to become the sole owner of the company. Although the Zweifler and Cerar valuations confirmed Turner's opinion, the court found that there were numerous defects in the valuation reports and that, as the plaintiffs alleged, the value of the company stock was far higher than the sale price. One of the defenses raised by the ESOP fiduciaries was that they had acted in good faith and that, therefore, they should not be held liable for breach of fiduciary duty even if the court disagreed with their conclusion as to the value of the shares held by the ESOP. The court rejected this defense for several reasons, including that the appraisers were not independent. The court found that Turner had for many years given advice to the Davis family concerning the family's control of the company and that his services relating to the transaction were directed at obtaining control of the company for Davis. The court found that Zweifler and Cerar were not independent because they were selected by Turner and Davis and dealt only with Turner and Davis. There was no evidence that either Zweifler or Cerar ever reported to, or conferred with, either of the two independent fiduciaries. Moreover, the court noted that the whole procedure adopted by the Aetna ESOP committee was flawed in that an independent valuation is not obtained by fixing a price and then obtaining appraisals to confirm that price. Rather, the court ruled that a prudent investigation must precede, not follow, the valuation of an ESOP asset. The court entered a judgment in favor of the plaintiff class and against Davis and the company's CFO, but it dismissed the claims against the independent fiduciaries.[268]

Q109 May ESOP appraisals be performed by the accountants for the plan sponsor?

The following example is evaluated in the IRS Manual Handbook:

> An employer maintaining an ESOP uses a large, national accounting firm for its auditing and tax requirements. The accounting firm proposes to use its valuation division to perform an appraisal for the ESOP. The valuation division is qualified to perform appraisals of the property and holds itself out to the public as an appraiser.

The audit guidelines provide that as long as the accounting firm's valuation division performs a majority of its appraisals for entities other than the employer maintaining the ESOP or entities related to that employer, the valuation division is an "independent appraiser" within the meaning of Section 401(a)(28)(C) of the Code.[269] The Department of Labor has not announced whether it would apply the same analysis in interpreting the independent appraiser requirement set forth in the proposed Department of Labor regulations.

Q110 To what extent is an ESOP trustee entitled to rely upon a valuation prepared by an independent appraiser?

To properly rely upon an independent appraisal, an ESOP trustee must read the valuation report and must make an effort to understand it. In particular, the trustee should verify that the information upon which the valuation is based is accurate and that the assumptions made by the appraiser make sense. In addition, the trustee should review the report carefully with the appraiser and verify that the methods used by the ap-

---

268. *Montgomery v. Aetna Plywood, Inc.*, 39 F. Supp.2d 915 (N.D. IL 1998) (other aspects of this case are discussed in Question 110, Example 2).
269. IRS Announcement 92-182, 49 I.R.B. 77 (1992).

praiser seem appropriate. Case law establishes that ESOP trustees will not be shielded from liability for paying too high a price for employer securities, or for selling employer securities at too low a price, where they passively accept valuation reports. As a federal court of appeals stated in one of the leading cases interpreting the adequate consideration exemption: "[a]n independent appraisal is not a magic wand that fiduciaries may simply wave over a transaction to ensure that their responsibilities are fulfilled."[270]

The courts acknowledge that an ESOP trustee does not need to become an expert in the valuation of closely held corporations. However, an ESOP trustee does not fulfill his or her fiduciary duty merely by hiring an independent appraiser. In addition, the trustee must (1) investigate the appraiser's qualifications, (2) provide the appraiser with complete and accurate information, and (3) make certain that reliance on the appraiser's advice is reasonably justified under the circumstances.[271]

> **Example 1.** In 1974, Edward Shay, the president and sole shareholder of Pacific Architects and Engineers, Inc. ("PAE"), sold approximately 40% of his PAE stock to an ESOP for a price of $10.67 per share. In 1988, Shay repurchased the shares from the ESOP at a price of $14.40 per share. The transaction was approved by Shay's two co-fiduciaries, both of whom worked for Shay as senior executives, based on an appraisal performed by Arthur Young, Inc. ("AY"). On the purchase and sale of the PAE stock, the ESOP earned a compound annual return of only 2.2%. The ESOP participants sued Shay and the other two fiduciaries for breach of fiduciary duty.
>
> In determining the value of the PAE stock, AY applied a series of discounts. First it applied a 60% discount to PAE's 50% interest in a joint venture that held Japanese real estate because the other 50% owner had more power and because Japanese real estate was over-

---

270. *Donovan v. Cunningham*, 716 F.2d 1455, 1474 (5th Cir. 1983), *cert. denied*, 476 U.S. 1251 (1984) (discussed in Question 106, Example 1).
271. *Howard v. Shay*, 100 F.3d 1484, (9th Cir. 1996); *Accord, Donovan v. Cunningham*, 716 F.2d 1455, (5th Cir. 1983) (discussed in Question 106, Example 1); *Lowen v. Tower Asset Management, Inc.*, 829 F.2d 1209, (2d Cir. 1987); and *Reich v. Valley Nat'l. Bank of Arizona*, 837 F. Supp. 1259 (S.D.N.Y. 1993) (discussed in Question 49, Example 2, and Question 51).

valued and volatile. Next, because the ESOP owned only 40% of the outstanding stock of PAE, AY applied a minority-interest discount of 40% to 50%. Finally, because there was no ready market in PAE stock, AY applied a 50% liquidity discount. By applying these discounts, AY calculated that although PAE had a net asset value of over $83 per share, the fair market value of the ESOP's stock was only $14.40 per share. Although AY provided reasons for applying the discounts, it did not provide empirical support for the amount of the discounts. The minority-interest and lack-of-marketability discounts both exceeded average discounts of these kinds. Moreover, AY cited the overvaluation and volatility of Japanese real estate in support of all three of its discounts. The court concluded that the ESOP fiduciaries should have questioned the valuation and sought explanations for the amounts of the discounts. Therefore, the court held that the ESOP fiduciaries had not fulfilled their fiduciary duties.[272]

Planning Pointer. If after a careful review of a valuation report and a discussion of the report with the appraiser, an ESOP trustee remains uncertain regarding whether the appraisal is appropriate, he or she then should retain a second independent appraisal firm to review the valuation.

Example 2. In 1992, the ESOP committee of the Aetna Plywood, Inc., Employee Stock Ownership Plan arranged for a sale by the ESOP of the company shares that it held. At that time, the ESOP held all of the outstanding shares of the company except for 17 shares held by the president of the company, Jeffrey G. Davis. Davis was one of the four members of the ESOP committee. After the ESOP sale, Davis became the sole shareholder of the company. A former employee of the company brought a class action against the members of the ESOP committee, charging that the price received by the ESOP for its shares was inadequate.

The court found that the price paid by the company for the shares held by the ESOP was far below their fair market value. Because the transaction involved self-dealing, in that it benefited Davis and resulted in his obtaining a controlling interest in the company, the

---

272. *Howard v. Shay*, 100 F.3d 1484 (9th Cir. 1996).

court noted that Davis had the burden of proving that he fulfilled his duties by, at a minimum, engaging in a careful investigation to ensure protection of the interests of the ESOP plan participants. The court noted that, although securing an independent valuation is evidence of a thorough investigation, it is not a "whitewash." The court found that the ESOP fiduciaries were not justified in relying upon the valuation report because it contained obvious errors that they should have discovered. The most obvious error was that in calculating the value of the ESOP stock on a per-share basis, the appraiser divided the enterprise value of the company by the number of authorized shares (100,000) rather than by the actual number of shares outstanding (84,411). Adjusting for this error alone increased the value of the ESOP shares by almost $2 million. Another error in the valuation report was a reduction in the valuation of the company by $6 million to reflect the projected ESOP repurchase liability. This adjustment was inappropriate because the stock redemption resulted in the elimination of this liability. The court also concluded that a marketability discount applied by the appraiser was inappropriate given the nature of the transaction.

The court concluded that these errors should have been discovered by the ESOP fiduciaries in the course of a conduct of a prudent investigation of the proposed transaction, and the court entered a judgment against the two ESOP committee members who were corporate officers, requiring them to pay over $5 million in damages to the plaintiff class, plus interest.[273] The court also ruled that the business appraisers retained by the ESOP committee were not independent. This aspect of the case is discussed above in Question 108.

Example 3. In 1990, Golden Financial Group, Inc. ("GFGI"), arranged for its wholly owned subsidiary, Hall Holding Company, to set up an ESOP. The primary asset of Hall Holding Company was stock of Hall Chemical Company. Hall Holding owned all of the outstanding shares of Hall Chemical. The Secretary of Labor brought an action against GFGI, certain of its officers, and the trustees of the ESOP (who also were officers of the company), alleging that they had breached their fiduciary duties by purchasing stock on behalf of the ESOP without

---

273. *Montgomery v. Aetna Plywood, Inc.*, 39 F. Supp. 2d 915 (N.D. IL 1998).

conducting an adequate investigation of the purchase and by overpaying for the stock. The district court granted summary judgment to the Secretary of Labor.[274]

On appeal, in an attempt to demonstrate a genuine issue of material fact sufficient to merit a trial, the defendants relied upon a valuation from a third-party appraiser. Although the Secretary of Labor did not dispute the appraiser's qualifications to value Hall Chemical, she argued that the fiduciaries were not justified in relying upon his appraisal because he had not been provided with complete and accurate information and because the fiduciaries had failed to verify that reliance upon his valuation was justified under the circumstances. The court of appeals affirmed the summary judgment in favor of the Department of Labor. In support of its ruling, the court noted that the appraiser's deposition testimony revealed that he had not been fully informed of all circumstances when he performed his valuation of Hall Chemical. In particular, he was not informed that the purpose of his valuation was to establish a value at which an ESOP would purchase a stake in Hall Holding. The appraiser acknowledged during his deposition that his valuation would have been different if he had been notified of this purpose, and he then would have applied a minority interest discount because the ESOP purchased only about 10% of the outstanding shares of Hall Holding. Moreover, the appraiser's valuation did not take into account an option that had been granted to the president of Hall Chemical to purchase 5% of its outstanding shares. Finally, the court noted that the appraiser valued Hall Chemical, not Hall Holding, and that his valuation of Hall Chemical was used to establish the value of Hall Holding. Although Hall Chemical was the major asset of Hall Holding, the court stated that Hall Chemical and Hall Holding were two different entities and that, therefore, since stock of Hall Holding was sold to the ESOP, Hall Holding should have been appraised, not Hall Chemical.

The defendants argued that the holding of the trial court should have been reversed and that the case should have been remanded for trial because they had reviewed the appraiser's draft valuation,

---

274. *Reich v. Hall Holding Co.*, 990 F. Supp. 995 (N.D. Oh. 1998) (also discussed in Question 120).

had discussed it with outside ERISA counsel, had recommended changes to the draft valuation, and had reviewed and discussed the final valuation among themselves and with outside ERISA counsel. The defendants argued that these facts raised a genuine issue as to whether they had conducted a prudent and independent investigation. However, the court of appeals ruled that because the appraiser's valuation was tainted by the fact that he was not provided with all of the information that he needed, and because the valuation of Hall Chemical was improperly applied to Hall Holding, it did not matter that the defendants had spent a great deal of time reviewing and recommending changes to the valuation. The court ruled that the defendants could not claim as a defense "that a great deal of time was spent reviewing and changing the valuation which was flawed from its inception and performed on the wrong company."[275]

For a discussion of this issue in the context of the ERISA prudence requirement, see Question 51.

Q111 What methods should an ESOP fiduciary employ to investigate a proposed purchase of employer securities?

In order to satisfy the prudence requirement in connection with a proposed purchase of employer securities, an ESOP fiduciary must engage in a diligent, independent investigation of the employer in order to ensure that the proposed investment is appropriate for the employees of the company, taking into account not only the proposed purchase price but also the risks inherent in the proposed investment.[276] What constitutes an appropriate investigation with respect to any particular proposed stock purchase will depend upon the facts and circumstances surrounding the

---

275. *Chao v. Hall Holding Co.*, 285 F. 3d 415, 431, n. 10 (6th Cir. 2002). *See also Keach v. U.S. Trust Co., N.A.*, 313 F. Supp. 2d 818, 868 (C.D. Ill. 2004), *aff'd*, 419 F.3d 626 (7th Cir. 2005) (extensive legal opinion limited to tax and ERISA compliance matters not sufficient) (discussed in Question 106, Example 4).

276. *Chao v. Hall Holding Co.*, 285 F. 3d 415 (6th Cir. 2002) (discussed in Question 110, Example 3, and in Question 120); *Howard v. Shay*, 100 F. 3d 1484, 1489 (9th Cir. 1996) (discussed in Question 110, Example 1); and *Reich v. Valley Nat'l. Bank of Arizona*, 837 F. Supp. 1259 (S.D.N.Y. 1993) (discussed in Question 49, Example 2, and Question 51).

particular transaction. However, in virtually all cases, an ESOP fiduciary should include the following steps as part of his or her analysis:

1. The trustee should review the plan and trust documents carefully so as to assure that he or she understands how the plan works and what his or her responsibilities are.
2. The trustee should investigate the business of the sponsoring employer. Among other things, the trustee should review the plan sponsor's financial statements, should visit the plan sponsor's main offices or plants, and should interview key corporate officers.
3. The trustee should assure that his or her financial adviser is independent and should carefully review the business valuation report prepared by his or her financial adviser.
4. The trustee should retain an independent law firm that has substantial experience in ESOP transactions for legal counseling. The trustee should direct his or her legal counsel to conduct a due-diligence investigation of the sponsoring employer's legal affairs, including a review of the sponsoring employer's corporate charter and bylaws, major contracts, title to real estate and other assets, and compliance with applicable laws and regulations. The trustee should review the results of the legal investigation with his or her legal counsel.
5. If the share purchase will be financed with the proceeds of a bank loan, the ESOP trustee should review the loan terms with his or her financial and legal advisors and verify that the loan terms will not be unduly burdensome for the sponsoring employer.
6. The trustee should be actively involved in negotiations over all of the terms and conditions of the proposed stock purchase, including the determination of the purchase price.

The above list is not meant to be exhaustive. A trustee should consider all factors that a knowledgeable investor would evaluate in considering whether to purchase stock of the sponsoring employer.

Planning Pointer. ESOP fiduciaries considering a purchase or sale of employer securities should not only conduct a thorough investigation of the proposed transaction but also carefully and thoroughly document their investigation. In particular, ESOP fiduciaries should take careful notes of their review of all valuation reports, of the questions that they present to the appraiser, and of the responses to their questions from the appraiser. In addition, careful minutes of all meetings of fiduciary committees should be maintained, again with a detailed focus on all discussions with the business appraiser.

Courts recognize that ESOP trustees must take cost considerations into account in determining the scope of an appropriate due diligence review.

Example. After the bankruptcy of Foster & Gallagher, Inc., in 2001, two participants in the company's ESOP brought an action against the ESOP trustee alleging that the trustee had breached its fiduciary duties in connection with the purchase of 30% of the company's outstanding shares for $70 million in 1995. At the trial, an accountant with Ernst & Young testified that the trustee's performance was deficient because it had failed to retain an independent accounting firm as part of the due-diligence team to review Foster & Gallagher's financial statements. The trustee had retained independent financial and legal advisors, both of which had extensive experience in ESOP transactions. The court stated that while hiring an independent CPA firm might be an advisable undertaking when considering a major stock purchase in an open-market transaction not involving an ESOP, this was not required in an ESOP transaction and that a qualified financial advisor's review of the financial statements complied with the standards and practices of prudent ESOP trustees. The court also noted that the accountant testified that his fees were approximately $350,000. As he was engaged only to review the due-diligence performed in connection with the 1995 ESOP transaction and did not perform the audit and financial review that he testified should have been done by a CPA firm, it appeared to the court that the kind of expert assistance that he recommended would be prohibitively expensive in many ESOP transactions.[277]

---

277. *Keach v. U.S. Trust Co., N.A.*, 313 F. Supp. 2d 818, 870 (C.D. Ill. 2004), *aff'd* 419 F.3d 626 (7th Cir. 2005) (also discussed in Question 106, Example 4).

Q112 What matters should an ESOP fiduciary direct legal counsel to investigate in connection with a proposed stock purchase?

In connection with a proposed purchase of employer securities, an ESOP fiduciary should request his or her legal counsel to review the employer's legal affairs. This investigation should be wide-ranging in scope and generally should include an investigation of the following matters:[278]

1. *Corporate Organizational Matters.* The employer's corporate charter, bylaws, minutes, and stock records should be reviewed. The states and foreign countries in which the employer conducts business should be determined, and appropriate qualification to do business in these jurisdictions should be verified.

2. *Tax Matters.* The employer's tax returns for all years for which the statute of limitations has not expired should be reviewed. Any past or pending tax audits should be investigated.

3. *Labor Relations.* Any collective bargaining agreements, and all agreements with the executives and consultants, should be reviewed. Employee manuals and handbooks and other personnel policies also should be investigated.

4. *Employee Benefit Plans.* All employee benefit plans and related trust agreements should be reviewed, together with related tax rulings and government filings.

5. *Real Estate.* A list of all real estate owned or leased by the employer should be obtained. The legal descriptions of all parcels of real estate owned by the employer should be reviewed, as well as all deeds, mortgages, and title insurance policies. Agreements relating to real property leases also should be reviewed.

6. *Other Property.* Information about machinery, equipment, and other important tangible personal property owned or leased by the employer should be obtained.

---

278. *See* Curtis and Granados, "Legal Due Diligence in ESOP Transactions," 22 *J. of Pension Plan. & Compliance* 18 (1996).

7. *Contracts.* All material contracts of the employer should be reviewed, including large purchase and sale orders, agreements with sales representatives, distribution agreements with suppliers and dealers, and loan or financing agreements (in addition to employment and other types of agreements referred to above). Copies of written product warranties also should be reviewed.

8. *Intellectual Property.* The employer's trademarks, copyrights, and patents should be reviewed, as well as pending applications for trademarks, copyrights, and patents. Licensing agreements, assignments, and trade secret agreements also should be reviewed, and information regarding infringement claims should be investigated.

9. *Insurance.* A description of the employer's insurance program should be obtained, and insurance policies should be reviewed.

10. *Litigation.* Information regarding all lawsuits or other controversies pending against the employer should be obtained, as well as information regarding recently settled controversies and facts that may reasonably be expected to give rise to claims in the future.

11. *Environmental Matters.* The employer's environmental records should be reviewed, and information should be obtained regarding hazardous materials used in the business and procedures for storing, transporting, and disposing hazardous substances. In most cases, a report from experienced environmental consultants should be obtained.

12. *Other Matters.* Depending on the nature of the employer's business, there may be other matters that require investigation, including, for example, required licenses and permits, political contributions, antitrust matters, and foreign-law considerations.

The ESOP fiduciary generally should obtain a written report from his or her legal advisor regarding the legal due-diligence investigations. The fiduciary should carefully review this report with the lawyers and then act appropriately in light of the information that has been obtained.

Q113 Should an ESOP fiduciary become involved in contract negotiations in connection with a proposed stock purchase?

After the ESOP fiduciary has completed an investigation of the kind described above in Questions 111 and 112, he or she then must take appropriate action in light of the information that has been obtained. This means that the ESOP fiduciary should actively participate in the negotiation of the price and terms of the stock purchase.[279] Information obtained in connection with the investigation of the employer should be applied in connection with determining what representations and warranties, closing conditions, and indemnification should be obtained to protect the employees. In addition, if previously undisclosed liabilities are discovered during the course of the investigation, it may be appropriate for the ESOP fiduciaries to negotiate for price concessions or escrow holdbacks.

Q114 What additional considerations should an ESOP fiduciary take into account in a multi-investor transaction?

In addition to the considerations described above that an ESOP fiduciary must take into account in evaluating the prudence of a proposed stock purchase, further concerns arise where other parties will be purchasing employer securities at the same time as the ESOP stock purchase. Then, in addition to assuring that the price paid by the ESOP does not exceed the fair market value of the securities and that the ESOP's interests are otherwise adequately protected, the fiduciary also must evaluate the fairness of the transaction to the ESOP as compared to other investors.[280] This requires the fiduciary to review not only the business and affairs of the employer but also all aspects of the transaction. The price to be paid by the ESOP should be compared to the price being paid by other parties to the transaction for their securities, and these prices should be

---

279. *Reich v. Valley Nat'l. Bank*, 837 F. Supp. 1259 (S.D.N.Y. 1993) (discussed in Question 45, Example 2, and Question 51).

280. Letter from Norman P. Goldberg, DOL Counsel for Fiduciary Litigation, Plan Benefits Security Division, to Charles R. Smith, Counsel to the Profit Sharing Committee of the Blue Bell, Inc. Savings, Profit Sharing and Retirement Plan (Nov. 23, 1984), *reprinted in* 12 Pens. Rep. (BNA) 52 (Jan. 7, 1985).

evaluated based on the expected rates of return and relative risks for the parties. Because of the complexities involved in evaluating the fairness of a multi-investor transaction where different parties acquire different kinds of employer securities, most ESOP consultants recommend that an independent fiduciary be retained to act on behalf of the ESOP in these types of transactions.[281]

Similar kinds of fairness considerations are presented where equity interests are awarded to key executives in connection or simultaneously with an ESOP transaction. These interests may take various forms, including stock options, stock bonuses, phantom stock awards, or stock appreciation rights. The benefits may be awarded to the executives either at the time of the ESOP stock purchase or at some later date, and they may be conditioned on satisfaction of various types of performance criteria. These kinds of arrangements should be analyzed by an ESOP fiduciary, with the assistance of its financial advisor, to assure that the ESOP is not subject to unfair dilution.[282]

Q115 Under what circumstances may an ESOP trustee sell stock of the plan sponsor?

As discussed in Question 14, the trustees of an ESOP must have *exclusive* authority and discretion over the management and control of the assets of the plan, except where they are subject to directions from another named fiduciary or where the authority to manage, acquire, or dispose of assets of the plan has been delegated to another fiduciary or to an investment manager. Unless one of these two exceptions applies, the decision whether to sell stock of a plan sponsor held by an ESOP is within the discretion of the ESOP trustees.

In determining whether to sell the plan sponsor's stock, the trustees must act in accordance with the exclusive-purpose requirement and must satisfy the prudence standard. In other words, ESOP trustees should sell the plan sponsor's stock only if a sale is in the best interests of the participants in the plan and if the terms and conditions of the sale are

---

281. *See* Report of the ERISA Advisory Council Ad Hoc Work Group on ESOPs, *The Participation of Leveraged Employee Stock Ownership Plans in Multi-Investor Leveraged Buyouts* (Nov. 12, 1987).

282. For further consideration of these issues, see the discussion in Question 44.

prudent. When applying these standards, ESOP trustees should also take into account the fact that the purpose of an ESOP is to *hold* employer securities. Since a sale of the plan sponsor's stock would be contrary to the purpose of an ESOP, the plan sponsor's stock should be sold only under unusual circumstances. In addition, if the offer comes from a related party, such as an officer or director of the plan sponsor or a major stockholder of the plan sponsor, then the sale must be for "adequate consideration." As discussed above in Question 93, the term "adequate consideration" generally means the fair market value of the stock.

The most common situation in which the stock of the plan sponsor is sold by an ESOP is in connection with a sale of the plan sponsor's business. Usually this will occur after the board of directors of the plan sponsor has made a determination that it is in the best interests of the plan sponsor and of its shareholders to sell the business. Although this decision falls within the scope of the authority of the board of directors of the plan sponsor, when a decision to sell has been made the ESOP trustees should verify that, in making this decision, the board has acted in a careful manner and free of conflicts of interests. As discussed above in Question 42, ESOP trustees are *not* required to independently evaluate business transactions properly authorized by corporate management. However, ESOP fiduciaries should monitor management to assure that the officers and directors of the plan sponsor are fulfilling their corporate fiduciary responsibilities, and they have a duty under ERISA to protect the interests of the plan participants where officers and directors of the plan sponsor violate their *corporate* fiduciary duties.

Another circumstance where it might be appropriate for ESOP fiduciaries to sell stock of the plan sponsor would be where the ESOP is being terminated. As discussed in Question 16, the sponsor of an ESOP generally has the right to terminate the plan, and it normally will be appropriate to sell the stock of the plan sponsor at the time of the plan termination. Other circumstances in which it might be appropriate for ESOP fiduciaries to sell stock of the plan sponsor include (1) situations where the value of the plan sponsor's stock is declining and can be expected to continue to decline and (2) where an offer to purchase the stock at a substantial premium is received. For discussions of the legal responsibilities of ESOP fiduciaries in these situations, see Questions 55 and 116.

Q116 If an ESOP trustee receives an offer to purchase stock of the plan sponsor at a price in excess of the appraised value of the stock, must the stock be sold?

As stated in Question 115, the purpose of an ESOP is to hold employer securities, not to buy and sell various assets with a view towards maximizing the investment return on a diversified asset portfolio. Moreover, as stated above in Question 55, an ESOP fiduciary who invests the assets of an ESOP in employer stock is entitled to a presumption that he or she has acted properly. Applying these principles, it is the general consensus of experienced ESOP consultants that ESOP fiduciaries are not required to sell employer securities merely because they receive a purchase offer at a price in excess of the most recent appraised value. In determining how to respond to an offer, ESOP fiduciaries should take into account the plan sponsor's prospects for the future and should consult with their independent financial advisor regarding projected future values of the plan sponsor's stock. Since the purpose of an ESOP is to hold employer securities, the stock normally should be sold only where a substantial premium is offered or where there are good reasons for selling the company (as discussed above in Question 115). One factor that the Department of Labor and the IRS take the position that ESOP fiduciaries should *not* consider in determining whether to sell stock of a plan sponsor is whether a sale might result in a loss of jobs for planned participants. Rather, according to the Department of Labor and the IRS, the fiduciaries must consider exclusively the financial interests of the participants in their future retirement income. *See* Question 30.

CHAPTER 5

Personal Liability

Contents

Q117 Can a fiduciary be held personally liable for a breach of duty? 134

Q118 Is a fiduciary liable for a breach not occurring during the fiduciary's term in office? 134

Q119 Is there a duty to remedy a fiduciary breach committed by a predecessor fiduciary? 135

Q120 What types of remedies can be imposed on a fiduciary for a breach of fiduciary duty? 136

Q121 What losses may a fiduciary be liable to restore? 137

Q122 What is the measure of a plan's loss to be restored as a remedy for a fiduciary breach? 137

Q123 Can any gains offset a loss resulting from a fiduciary's breach? 139

Q124 What profits may a fiduciary be liable to give up? 139

Q125 What types of equitable remedies have been applied in ESOP cases? 139

Q126 What is the 20% penalty for breach of fiduciary duty? 141

Q127 What excise taxes and other penalties may apply to a fiduciary breach? 141

Q128 May a fiduciary face criminal liability for a breach of fiduciary duty? 142

Q129 Are there other laws imposing criminal liability on a fiduciary? 142

Q130 Do any federal crimes specifically apply to employee benefit plans? 142

Q131 May a fiduciary face civil liability for interference with rights protected under ERISA? 143

Q117 Can a fiduciary be held personally liable for a breach of duty?

Yes. A fiduciary who breaches the fiduciary requirements of ERISA is personally liable for any losses to the plan resulting from the breach. Any profits obtained by the fiduciary through the use of plan assets must be restored to the plan.[283] A civil action may be brought by a participant or beneficiary or by another fiduciary.[284] However, a plaintiff who seeks to hold a fiduciary personally liable for breach of fiduciary duty must establish a casual connection between the alleged breach and the alleged loss.[285] The court may impose other appropriate relief, including removal of the fiduciary.[286]

Q118 Is a fiduciary liable for a breach not occurring during the fiduciary's term in office?

A fiduciary cannot be held liable for a breach of duty committed before he or she became a fiduciary or after he or she ceased to be a fiduciary.

---

283. ERISA § 409(a).

284. ERISA § 502(a)(2). In *McBride v. PLM Int'l., Inc.*, 179 F.3d 737 (9th Cir. 1999), the Ninth Circuit held that a *former* participant in an ESOP could bring an action under ERISA where he had been terminated in retaliation for his opposition to the defendant's proposed termination of the plan. The court held that if an employee is a participant at the time of the alleged ERISA violation and alleges that he was discharged or discriminated against because of protected whistleblowing activities, he has standing to sue under ERISA. The court stated that to require the claimant to be a participant at the time of filing suit would undermine the purpose of the "whistleblower" provisions of ERISA, which the court stated to be "to provide a federal remedy for discrimination against plan participants for exercising their protected rights under ERISA." 179 F.3d at 743.

285. *Henry v. Champlain Enterprises, Inc.*, 288 F. Supp. 2d 202, at 230 (N.D.N.Y. 2003) (allegation that ESOP fiduciaries had breached their responsibilities by failing to enforce a contractual right dismissed where plaintiffs failed to specifically allege any loss derived from the failure by the fiduciaries to invoke the contractual right). See also *Kuper v. Iovenko*, 66 F.3d 1447 (6th Cir. 1995) (discussed in Question 55, Example 2); and *Keach v. U.S. Trust Co., N.A.*, 313 F. Supp. 2d 818, 873 (C.D. Ill. 2004), *aff'd*, 419 F.3d 626 (7th Cir. 2005) (discussed in Question 106, Example 4, and in Question 111).

286. ERISA § 409(a).

Rather, a person can be held liable only for a breach committed while acting as a fiduciary.[287] However, as discussed in Question 52, if a fiduciary resigns without providing for continuing management of the plan, the act of resignation may constitute a breach of fiduciary duty.[288]

> **Example.** James and Raymon Mortell were the trustees of a profit-sharing plan sponsored by the Mortell Company, of which James and Raymon were shareholders. The profit-sharing plan owned shares of the company's stock. In order to make the company eligible for the subchapter S election for federal income tax purposes, James and Raymon arranged for the profit-sharing plan to sell its shares of company stock back to the company. On April 15, 1983, James and Raymon resigned as trustees of the profit-sharing plan, and a bank was named as successor trustee. On April 20, 1983, the successor trustee accepted the company's offer to purchase the shares of the company held in the plan. Before accepting the offer, the successor trustee conducted an investigation and analysis of the proposed transaction, including reviewing a valuation report that concluded that the purchase price was equal to the fair market value of the shares. Present and former employees of the company brought an action against James and Raymon and against the successor trustee, alleging breach of fiduciary duty in connection with the sale of the company stock. The court held that, because James and Raymon had resigned as trustees on April 15, 1983 and did not carry out any fiduciary functions after that date, they could not be held liable for the successor trustee's acceptance on April 20, 1983 of an offer to purchase the company stock held by the plan.[289]

Q119 Is there a duty to remedy a fiduciary breach committed by a predecessor fiduciary?

Yes. If a successor fiduciary learns of a breach committed by a predecessor, the successor is obligated to take reasonable steps to remedy the situa-

---

287. ERISA § 409(b).
288. *Freund v. Marshall & Ilsley Bank*, 485 F. Supp. 629, 641 (W.D. Wis. 1979).
289. *Anderson v. Mortell*, 722 F. Supp. 462 (N.D. Ill. 1989).

tion as successor fiduciary. Failure to take remedial action constitutes a separate, current breach of fiduciary duty by the successor.[290]

Q120 What types of remedies can be imposed on a fiduciary for a breach of fiduciary duty?

A fiduciary found to be in breach of his or her duty under ERISA is subject to legal remedies, equitable remedies, or both. Legal remedies include money damages for restoration of plan losses or disgorgement of the fiduciary's profits.[291] Equitable remedies under ERISA specifically endorsed by its legislative history include injunctions, constructive trusts, and removal of a fiduciary.[292]

> *Example.* In 1990, the trustees of the Hall Chemical Company ESOP purchased approximately 10% of the outstanding shares of the plan sponsor's parent corporation, Hall Holding Company, for $3.5 million. The Secretary of Labor brought an action against Hall

---

290. DOL Adv. Op. Ltr. No. 76-95 (Sept. 30, 1976).
291. ERISA § 409(a); *Mertens v. Hewitt Assocs.*, 508 U.S. 248 (1993) (restoration of losses is not an equitable remedy). See *Montgomery v. Aetna Plywood, Inc.*, 39 F. Supp. 2d 915 (N.D. IL 1998) (judgment against ESOP committee members in excess of $5 million, plus interest) (discussed in Questions 108 and 110, Example 2).
292. S. Rep. No. 383, 93d Cong., 1st Sess., 105–106 (1973); *See, e.g., Montgomery v. Aetna Plywood, Inc.*, 39 F. Supp. 2d 915 (N.D. IL 1998) (removing and barring ESOP committee members from any fiduciary relationship with a profit sharing plan that was the successor to an ESOP) (discussed in Questions 108 and 110, Example 2); *Eaves v. Penn*, 587 F.2d 453 (10th Cir. 1978) (discussed in Question 125); and *Dairy Fresh Corp. v. Poole*, 108 F. Supp. 2d 1344 (S.D. Ala. 2000) (corporation removed as administrator of its ESOP and as ESOP trustee for a breach of fiduciary duties in connection with an attempted reformation of an ESOP that would have reduced the amount of company stock held by the ESOP by 50%); *Amalgamated Clothing & Textile Workers Union, AFL-CIO v. Murdock*, 861 F.2d 1406 (9th Cir. 1988) (constructive trust); *Katsaros v. Cody*, 744 F.2d 270 (2d Cir 1984), *cert. denied*, 469 U.S. 1072 (1984) (removal, with appointment of new investment managers and other trustees for fifteen months); and *Whitfield v. Tomasso*, 682 F. Supp. 1289 (E.D.N.Y. 1988) (permanent injunction against acting as fiduciary of, or providing service to, any ERISA plan).

Holding Company, several of its officers, and the ESOP trustees (who were employees of Hall Holding Company) alleging that they had breached their fiduciary duties by causing the ESOP to pay more than fair market value for the stock. The district court granted summary judgment on behalf of the Secretary of Labor and found that the price paid by the ESOP for the stock exceeded the fair market value of the stock by approximately $1,050,000, which amount, together with prejudgment interest of approximately $1.2 million, was awarded to the participants in the ESOP. The court ordered the defendants to pay the award to the participants, with the award allocated based upon the amounts of stock that had been received or would be received by the participants in the future.[293]

Q121 What losses may a fiduciary be liable to restore?

A fiduciary may be liable to restore the entire amount of any loss suffered by the plan resulting from the fiduciary's breach of duty. If the fiduciary's breach does not result in a monetary loss to the plan, ordinarily there is no damage award as a remedy for the breach, although equitable remedies may be imposed on the fiduciary.[294]

Q122 What is the measure of a plan's loss to be restored as a remedy for a fiduciary breach?

A plan's loss caused by a fiduciary's breach of duty is measured by comparing what the plan actually earned (or lost) as a result of the fiduciary's actions with what the plan would hypothetically have earned (or lost) had the fiduciary's actions not taken place. Where several hypothetical alternatives are available, a court should use the alternative most favorable to the affected participants and beneficiaries.

---

293. *Reich v. Hall Holding Co.*, 990 F. Supp. 955 (N.D. Oh. 1998), *aff'd sub nom Chao v. Hall Holding Co.*, 285 F. 3d 415 (6th Cir. 2002) (also discussed in Question 110, Example 3).

294. ERISA § 409(a); *Donovan v. Cunningham*, 716 F.2d 1455 (5th Cir. 1983), *cert. denied*, 467 U.S. 1251 (1984) (discussed in Question 106, Example 1).

Example. In 1981, LTV made a tender offer for a controlling interest in Grumman Corporation at a price of $45 per share. The plan owned 525,000 shares of Grumman stock. The trustees of the plan, who also were officers of Grumman, determined not to tender any of the plan's shares, and they used plan funds to purchase 1,158,000 additional shares of Grumman stock at the prevailing market price of $36 to $39.75 a share (the price having risen from $26.75 per share to $35.88 per share when the tender offer was announced). The tender offer was preliminarily enjoined in court, and it ultimately failed. Grumman stock dropped in price to approximately the pre-tender offer level of $23 per share. Approximately 17 months after the stock was purchased, the trustees, with court permission, sold the newly purchased stock (and some of the prior holdings) for $47.55 per share, realizing a $13 million gain. The court held that the plan nevertheless might have sustained a loss, and it remanded the case to the district court for a determination of the whether a loss had been incurred. The measure of loss required a comparison of (1) what the plan actually earned on the investment in Grumman stock with (2) what the plan would have earned had the funds been available for other plan purposes. If (1) was less than (2), the difference was the loss; if (1) was not less than (2), there was no loss.[295]

Where ESOP fiduciaries are found to have paid more than fair market value for shares of employer stock, the amount of the overpayment constitutes a compensable loss to the plan. The amount of the loss is the difference between what the ESOP paid for the stock and the fair market value of the stock at the time of the transaction, plus interest.[296] In some cases, ESOP fiduciaries have contended that with a value of the stock acquired by the ESOP increases after the transaction, participants can

---

295. *Donovan v. Bierwirth*, 754 F.2d 1049 (2d Cir. 1985) (other aspects of this case are discussed in Question 49, Example 1).
296. *Horn v. McQueen*, 215 F. Supp. 2d 867 (W.D. Ky. 2002) (discussed in Question 106, Example 3); *Reich v. Hall Holding Co.*, 990 F. Supp. 955 (N.D. Oh. 1998), *aff'd sub nom. Chao v. Hall Holding Co.*, 285 F. 3d 415 (6th Cir. 2002) (discussed in Question 110, Example 3); and *Reich v. Valley Nat'l. Bank*, 837 F. Supp. 1259 (S.D.N.Y. 1993) (discussed in Question 49, Example 2, and in Question 51).

show no loss to the plan even if the ESOP paid too much for the stock. However, the courts have uniformly rejected this argument.[297]

Q123 Can any gains offset a loss resulting from a fiduciary's breach?

Generally, no. Losses to the plan resulting from a transaction constituting a breach of fiduciary duty are not offset by gains resulting from any separate and distinct transaction.

> *Example.* The administrator of a profit sharing plan caused the plan to invest in three entities in which he and other fiduciaries made substantial investments before and after the plan invested in the three entities. The administrator and the other fiduciaries profited from the plan's investment. Viewed as a portfolio, the plan's investment in the three entities yielded 72%—a very favorable yield. Two of the three investments had very high yields; one yielded only 4%. The court ruled that plan participants were entitled to compare the 4% yield with hypothetical earnings on alternative investments. The shortfall of $6,700 constituted a loss under Section 409(a) of ERISA, without offset by the substantial gain on the two other investments.[298]

Q124 What profits may a fiduciary be liable to give up?

If a fiduciary uses plan assets in a breach of fiduciary duty and makes any profit as a result, the fiduciary must give up those profits, regardless of whether or not the plan suffered a loss.[299]

Q125 What types of equitable remedies have been applied in ESOP cases?

Equitable remedies that have been applied by courts in cases involving ESOPs include the following:

---

297. Id.
298. *Leigh v. Engle*, 669 F. Supp. 1390, 1405 (N.D. Ill. 1987), *on remand from* 727 F.2d 113 (7th Cir. 1984), *aff'd*, 858 F.2d 361 (7th Cir. 1988), *cert. denied*, 489 U.S. 1078 (1989) (discussed above in Question 27, Example 2).
299. ERISA § 409(a).

1. rescission of a purchase of employer securities by an ESOP;[300]
2. removal of management trustees and the appointment of a neutral trustee in their place;[301] and
3. permanently enjoining persons from acting as fiduciaries for, or providing any services to, any employee benefit plans.[302]

Example. In 1975, Ralph W. Penn entered into an agreement to acquire all of the outstanding shares of Glen's, Inc., a corporation engaged in the restaurant business, from Glen R. Eaves and his wife, Alleen. The purchase price was approximately $1 million. The agreement provided for a substantial portion of the purchase price to be paid out of funds in the company's profit-sharing plan. Mr. and Mrs. Eaves resigned as officers and directors of the company and as fiduciaries of the profit-sharing plan on the closing date. Penn succeeded them as trustee of the plan and converted it into an ESOP. After Penn took control of the company and of the plan, he caused the company to contribute $491,000 to the plan, $215,000 of which was drawn from the company's operating capital and liquid assets and $275,000 of which was obtained from a bank. As trustee of the plan, Penn then used the $491,000 contribution to the plan and the plan's preexisting assets of approximately $520,000 to pay the Eaves for 97% of the stock of the company. Penn personally purchased the remaining 3% of the shares for $25,000, which he borrowed from the company.

As a result of the cash contribution to the plan, the value of the company's shares was reduced by approximately $500,000. The effect of that contribution, combined with Penn's mismanagement of the

---

300. *Eaves v. Penn*, 426 F. Supp. 830 (W.D. Okla. 1976), *aff'd*, 587 F.2d 453 (10th Cir. 1978).
301. *Shoen v. AMERCO*, 885 F. Supp. 1332 (D. Nev. 1994) (during a proxy contest, the management trustees improperly advised the participants to direct the voting of the shares allocated to their accounts in favor of management) (discussed in Question 27, Example 3).
302. *Martin v. Feilen*, 965 F.2d 660 (8th Cir. 1992), *cert. denied*, 113 S.Ct. 1979 (1993) (discussed above in Question 27, Example 1); *Martin v. Harline*, 15 EBC (BNA) 1138 (D. Utah 1992) (discussed in Question 17).

company, caused the company to suffer severe financial reverses. The Secretary of Labor brought an action against Mr. Penn and Mr. and Mrs. Eaves, alleging that they had violated their fiduciary duties under ERISA. The court found that all three defendants had violated their fiduciary duties and ordered a rescission of the sale of stock of the company to the plan, restoration of income and profits lost to the plan, and the appointment of a new trustee.[303]

Q126 What is the 20% penalty for breach of fiduciary duty?

A penalty of 20% of the amount payable pursuant to a court order or settlement agreement with the Department of Labor is assessed by the Department of Labor for breach of fiduciary duty. The penalty may be waived or reduced if the fiduciary (1) acted reasonably and in good faith, or (2) cannot otherwise be reasonably expected to be able to restore all plan losses without severe financial hardship.[304] The penalty is reduced by the amount of any penalty or tax imposed with respect to a prohibited transaction under Sections 406 and 502(i) of ERISA or Section 4975 of the Code.[305]

Q127 What excise taxes and other penalties may apply to a fiduciary breach?

A breach of fiduciary duty may also constitute a prohibited transaction under Section 406 of ERISA, Section 4975 of the Code, or both. Section 4975 of the Code imposes upon the disqualified persons an excise tax equal to 15% of the amount involved in the prohibited transaction for each year or part of a year in which the transaction remains uncorrected. An additional tax equal to 100% of the amount involved is imposed upon the disqualified persons if the prohibited transaction is not corrected.[306] See Question 79.

---

303. *Eaves v. Penn*, 426 F. Supp. 830 (W.D. Okla 1976), *aff'd*, 587 F.2d 453 (10th Cir. 1978).
304. ERISA § 502(l)(3); Prop. DOL Reg. § 2560.502(i)-1.
305. ERISA § 502(l)(4).
306. Code § 4975(a), (b); ERISA § 502(i); DOL Reg. § 2560.502i-1.

Q128 May a fiduciary face criminal liability for a breach of fiduciary duty?

Yes. Any person who willfully violates any reporting or disclosure provision in Title I of ERISA is subject to a fine of $5,000 (or $100,000 in the case of a partnership or corporation), imprisonment for one year, or both.[307] An intentional violation of the prohibition against service as a fiduciary (among other positions) to an employee benefit plan by any person convicted of any offense specified in Section 411(a) of ERISA is subject to a fine of $10,000, imprisonment for five years, or both.[308]

Q129 Are there other laws imposing criminal liability on a fiduciary?

Yes. The use of force or violence, or the threat of force or violence, or the use of fraud to restrain, coerce, or intimidate any participant or beneficiary in order to interfere with or prevent the exercise of any right under an employee benefit plan may result in a $10,000 fine, imprisonment for one year, or both.[309]

Q130 Do any federal crimes specifically apply to employee benefit plans?

Yes. Accepting kickbacks in connection with an ERISA plan is a federal crime punishable by a $10,000 fine, three years' imprisonment, or both.[310] Knowingly making a false statement or knowingly concealing facts in connection with plan documents required by ERISA is a federal crime punishable by a $10,000 fine, five years' imprisonment, or both.[311] Embezzling plan assets from an employee pension or welfare plan, as defined in ERISA, is a federal crime punishable by a $10,000 fine, five years' imprisonment, or both.[312]

---

307. ERISA § 501.
308. ERISA § 411(b).
309. ERISA § 511.
310. 18 U.S.C. § 1954.
311. 18 U.S.C. § 1027.
312. 18 U.S.C. § 664.

Q131 May a fiduciary face civil liability for interference with rights protected under ERISA?

Yes, if the fiduciary is the employer. Participants or beneficiaries may recover against any person who interferes with the exercise or attainment of any right to which they are entitled under a plan or ERISA. Interference can include discharges, fines, suspensions, discipline, or discrimination against the participants or beneficiaries.[313] This liability is generally applied to employers that discharge employees with the intent to cut off vesting under a retirement plan, and a number of courts have expressly limited this liability to employers.[314]

> *Example.* An employer discharged a 62-year old employee a few weeks before his qualified retirement plan benefits would have become vested. The proximity of the termination date and the vesting date was sufficient to infer that the employer's purpose in discharging the employee was to deprive him of his retirement benefits. The discharge was a violation of Section 510 of ERISA, even though it did not constitute age discrimination.[315]

---

313. ERISA § 510; *Ingersoll-Rand Co. v. McClendon*, 498 U.S. 133 (1990).

314. *Byrd v. MacPapers, Inc.*, 961 F.2d 157 (11th Cir. 1992); *West v. Butler*, 621 F.2d 240 (6th Cir. 1980).

315. *Hazen Paper Co. v. Biggins*, 507 U.S. 604 (1993), *vacating Biggins v. Hazen Paper Co.*, 953 F.2d 1405 (1st Cir. 1992) (vacated only as to age discrimination).

CHAPTER 6

Protecting Against the Risk of Liability

Contents

Q132	May a plan release a fiduciary from liability?	146
Q133	May a fiduciary be relieved from his or her fiduciary duties by delegating duties with respect to a plan to another individual?	147
Q134	May a plan fiduciary indemnify its employees who actually perform the fiduciary services for the plan?	147
Q135	May a plan purchase insurance for itself or for plan fiduciaries to cover liabilities or losses resulting from the acts or omissions of plan fiduciaries?	147
Q136	May a fiduciary or an employer purchase insurance for the plan fiduciary to cover liability or losses resulting from the acts or omissions of the plan fiduciary?	148
Q137	What losses are covered by a typical fiduciary liability insurance policy?	148
Q138	Who is typically covered under a fiduciary liability insurance policy?	149
Q139	What is the difference between an ERISA bond, employee benefits liability insurance, and fiduciary liability insurance?	149
Q140	What policy limits are appropriate?	149
Q141	May an employer who sponsors an ESOP indemnify a fiduciary?	149
Q142	May a plan reimburse a fiduciary's legal expenses incurred in defending a lawsuit charging breach of fiduciary duties?	151
Q143	If a fiduciary is found liable for breaching his or her fiduciary duties, can the fiduciary be held liable for attorneys' fees?	151
Q144	May attorneys' fees be recovered by a defendant in an ERISA action?	152

145

Q132 May a plan release a fiduciary from liability?

In general, no. Provisions in a plan or other agreement that would relieve a fiduciary of liability for breaching the fiduciary liability rules ("exculpatory provisions") are void as against public policy. These kinds of provisions would relieve the fiduciary of responsibility to the plan by abrogating the plan's right to recovery from the fiduciary for breaching his or her fiduciary obligations.[316] This prohibition, however, does not prevent a fiduciary from allocating or delegating his or her responsibilities.[317] (See Questions 11 and 133.) Further, a fiduciary may be indemnified (i.e., repaid or insured against loss) by a person or entity other than the plan, as described in Questions 141 and 142.

> *Planning Pointer.* A statement in a plan document that a fiduciary has no liability resulting from any action he or she takes with respect to a plan is void. Also, the plan cannot indemnify a fiduciary against fiduciary liabilities. However, a statement that another fiduciary is responsible for certain fiduciary duties is valid.
>
> *Example.* A provision in a trust agreement between a company that sponsors an ESOP and the ESOP trustee provided that the ESOP would indemnify the trustee for any liability the trustee would incur in responding to tender offers as long as the trustee precisely followed the plan participants' directions. In a case brought by the Department of Labor, the court ruled that this indemnification agreement was not valid because it created an incentive for the trustee to breach its fiduciary duties to act in the best interests of the ESOP participants, since the trustee would be unprotected by the indemnification provisions if the trustee did not precisely follow the participants' direction.[318]

---

316. ERISA § 410(a). *See Delta Star, Inc. v. Patton*, 76 F. Supp. 2d 617 (W.D. PA 1999) (discussed in Question 44).
317. ERISA Conf. Comm. Rep. at p. 5101.
318. *Martin v. NationsBank of Georgia, N.A.*, 16 EBC (BNA) 2138 (N.D. Ga. 1993) (other aspects of this case are discussed in Question 69).

Q133 May a fiduciary be relieved from his or her fiduciary duties by delegating duties with respect to a plan to another individual?

Yes. Although ERISA prohibits exculpatory provisions in a plan, a fiduciary may, under certain conditions, delegate duties to other individuals and be freed from responsibility for the other persons' breach of duties. However, a trustee may not allocate or delegate his or her responsibility to manage and control plan assets.

Fiduciary duties may be allocated or delegated pursuant to authority contained in the plan document authorizing the allocation or delegation. Certain fiduciary duties may be allocated among named fiduciaries, and a named fiduciary may designate persons other than named fiduciaries to carry out certain fiduciary duties (if the plan expressly provides procedures for allocation or designation).[319] If the plan instrument does not provide for a procedure for the allocation of fiduciary responsibilities among named fiduciaries, any allocation that the named fiduciaries may make among themselves will not relieve a named fiduciary of liability for the performance of fiduciary responsibilities allocated to other named fiduciaries.[320]

Q134 May a plan fiduciary indemnify its employees who actually perform the fiduciary services for the plan?

Yes. This indemnification is permissible because it does not relieve the fiduciary of responsibility or liability under ERISA.[321]

Q135 May a plan purchase insurance for itself or for plan fiduciaries to cover liabilities or losses resulting from the acts or omissions of plan fiduciaries?

Yes. However, the insurance contract must permit recourse by the insurer against the fiduciary for the loss resulting from a breach of a fiduciary obligation by the fiduciary.[322]

---

319. ERISA § 405(c)(1). See discussion in Question 11.
320. DOL Reg. § 2509.75-8 at FR-13. For a thorough discussion of the rules regarding allocating and delegating fiduciary responsibilities, see Fiduciary Answer Book, ch 4.
321. DOL Reg. § 2509.75-4.
322. ERISA § 410(b).

Note. An issue that is unresolved is whether fiduciary liability insurance may cover fiduciaries for the 20% excise tax for fiduciary breaches under Section 502(l) of ERISA.

The fiduciary who is involved in purchasing insurance against fiduciary breaches for the plan must do his or her best to secure the most suitable coverage for the plan at no greater expenditure of plan assets than is necessary.[323]

Q136 May a fiduciary or an employer purchase insurance for the plan fiduciary to cover liability or losses resulting from the acts or omissions of the plan fiduciary?

Yes. A fiduciary may purchase insurance to cover his or her liability resulting from a breach of fiduciary duties, and an employer may purchase insurance for the plan fiduciary. Moreover, in this case (unlike the situation where the *plan* purchases the policy), the policy need not provide for recourse against the fiduciary.[324]

Q137 What losses are covered by a typical fiduciary liability insurance policy?

There is no standard form of fiduciary liability insurance policy, but most of these policies cover losses, up to the policy limit, incurred by reason of "wrongful acts." The term "wrongful act" generally is defined as follows: (1) any breach of the duties imposed by ERISA upon the fiduciaries of an insured plan; (2) any other claim brought against the plan sponsor or a plan fiduciary by reason of fiduciary services; and (3) any negligent act, error, or omission arising solely in connection with the administration of the insured plan. Losses covered typically include compensatory damages, settlements paid, and defense costs. Taxes, civil or criminal fines, and penalties may be deemed uninsurable under applicable laws.[325]

---

323. DOL Interp. Bull. No. 75-4 (June 4, 1975).

324. ERISA § 410(b).

325. The author gratefully acknowledges the assistance of Jeffrey Gelburd, of Murray Risk Management and Insurance, for his assistance in the preparation of Questions 137 through 140.

Q138 Who is typically covered under a fiduciary liability insurance policy?

The insured parties under a fiduciary-liability insurance policy usually include (1) the plan sponsor, (2) the plan itself, and (3) persons serving as fiduciaries with respect to the plan.

Q139 What is the difference between an ERISA bond, employee benefits liability insurance, and fiduciary liability insurance?

Sponsors of employee benefit plans are required under ERISA to provide bonds that protect the plans against losses by reason of thefts of plan assets by a plan administrator, a trustee, or another fiduciary. Employee benefits liability insurance normally is included within a plan sponsor's general liability policy and covers errors and omissions in connection with the administration of the plan. Fiduciary liability insurance provides protection against actions involving allegations of breach of fiduciary duty in connection with the administration of a plan.

Q140 What policy limits are appropriate?

The amount of coverage to be obtained for any particular fiduciary liability insurance policy will depend upon the facts and circumstances relating to that plan. However, there are two important factors that always should be considered. First, the payment of defense costs, such as legal expenses, normally will count against the policy limits. Therefore, coverage should be sufficient to cover not only any possible judgment, but also anticipated legal and other defense costs. Second, it should be determined whether claims under other insurance policies carried by the plan sponsor might reduce the limits under the fiduciary policy.

Q141 May an employer who sponsors an ESOP indemnify a fiduciary?

Yes. Although ERISA prohibits the indemnification and exculpation of a fiduciary by an employee benefit plan, ERISA permits the indemnification of the fiduciary by an employer who sponsors the plan. This indemnification does not relieve the fiduciary of responsibility or liability for fiduciary breaches. Rather, this indemnification leaves the fiduciary fully responsible and liable, but permits another party to satisfy any liability incurred by the fiduciary. Therefore, this indemnification is not void as against public policy under Section 410 of ERISA.[326] However, there is some question whether indemnification by the sponsor of an ESOP is appropriate where the ESOP holds all of the outstanding shares of the company.[327] In that case, the full economic burden of the indemnification falls upon the participants in the plan.

Note. An issue that is not resolved is whether a fiduciary may obtain indemnity from an employer for the 20% civil penalty assessed under Section 502(l) of ERISA. Since the purpose of the 20% mandatory penalty for fiduciary breaches is to deter violations of the fiduciary responsibility provisions, the payment of the penalty arguably must be borne by the individual who incurred the breach.

---

326. DOL Reg. § 2509.75-4.

327. In one of the oldest ESOP cases, a federal district court held that where an ESOP owns a substantial portion of the sponsoring company's stock, it would be inconsistent with the intentions of ERISA to allow a trustee who has breached his or her fiduciary duties to the ESOP to be indemnified by the sponsoring company, because the ESOP indirectly would bear the financial burden of the indemnification. *Donovan v. Cunningham*, 541 F. Supp. 276, 289 (S.D. Tex. 1982), *aff'd in part, vacated in part, and rev'd in part on other grounds*, 716 F.2d 1455 (5th Cir. 1983), *cert. denied*, 467 U.S. 1251 (1984) (discussed in Question 106, Example 1). *Accord, Delta Star, Inc. v. Patton*, 76 F. Supp. 2d 617, 640 (W.D. Pa. 1999) (discussed in Question 44). However, the holdings in these cases appear to be limited to situations in which ESOP trustees have been held liable for breach of fiduciary duty. The Court of Appeals for the Seventh Circuit has held that an ESOP trustee may be indemnified for costs incurred in connection with the defense of a claim of breach of fiduciary duty where the trustee is exonerated. *Packer Engineering, Inc. v. Kratoville*, 965 F.2d 174 (7th Cir. 1992). In that case, the court asked rhetorically "[h]ow could anyone take seriously the proposition that ERISA forbids the indemnification of fiduciaries wrongly accused of misconduct, when ERISA itself allows a court to award fees to the prevailing side?" *Id.* at 176. *See also Pudela v. Swanson*, 1995 U.S. Dist. LEXIS 2148 (N.D. Ill.) (denial of motion by ESOP participants for summary judgment on argument that provisions of plan sponsor's bylaws indemnifying ESOP fiduciaries was invalid).

Q142 May a plan reimburse a fiduciary's legal expenses incurred in defending a lawsuit charging breach of fiduciary duties?

Yes. A plan can provide for reimbursing a fiduciary or for advancing funds to the fiduciary to enable the fiduciary to defend against a claim that he or she breached fiduciary duties. This kind of a provision does not violate Section 410(a) of ERISA if the indemnification agreement also provides that if a court ultimately determines that the fiduciary breached his or her fiduciary duties, the fiduciary will be required to reimburse the plan for the advances along with reasonable interest.[328] However, the Department of Labor has ruled that a broad plan provision that authorizes the reimbursement of legal fees incurred by a fiduciary in any lawsuit arising in the performance of his duties would violate Section 410(a) of ERISA.[329]

Q143 If a fiduciary is found liable for breaching his or her fiduciary duties, can the fiduciary be held liable for attorneys' fees?

Yes. A court may, in its discretion, award reasonable attorneys' fees and costs in a litigation claiming breach of fiduciary duties under ERISA. Courts generally consider the following factors in deciding whether to award fees and costs:

1. the degree of the offending parties' bad faith;
2. the offending parties' ability to pay an award of fees;
3. whether an award of fees would have a deterrent effect on others in similar circumstances;

---

328. DOL Adv. Op. Ltr. No. 77-66/67A (Sept. 9, 1977); *Packer Eng'g Inc. v. Kratoville*, 965 F.2d 174 (7th Cir. 1992) (where a plan provided for the indemnification of fiduciaries for all expenses incurred in the course of the performance of their duties, the plan fiduciary was entitled to compensation for expenses incurred in successfully defending himself against claims that he violated his fiduciary duties).

329. DOL Adv. Op. Ltr. No. 78-29 (Dec. 1, 1978).

4. whether the action benefited all plan participants or the action was brought to resolve a significant legal question regarding ERISA; and

5. the relative merits of the parties' positions.[330]

No one factor is determinative.[331]

Q144 May attorneys' fees be recovered by a defendant in an ERISA action?

Yes. A court may, in its discretion, award reasonable attorneys' fees to either party in ERISA litigation. The majority of circuit courts apply the same five-factor approach in determining entitlement to attorney fees to defendants as they do to plaintiffs.[332]

---

330. *Gray v. New England Tel. & Tel. Co.*, 792 F.2d 251, 257–58 (1st Cir. 1986); *Eaves v. Penn*, 587 F.2d 453 (10th Cir. 1978) (discussed in Question 125).

331. *Bishop v. Osborn Transp., Inc.*, 687 F. Supp. 1526 (N.D. Ala. 1988).

332. *See Gray v. New England Tel. & Tel. Co.*, 792 F.2d 251 (1st Cir. 1986).

About the Author

David Ackerman is a partner in the Employee Benefits and Executive Compensation Practice of Morgan, Lewis & Bockius. Mr. Ackerman co-chairs the Morgan Lewis ESOP team, which is one of the largest groups of ESOP lawyers in the country.

Mr. Ackerman is one of the most knowledgeable ESOP lawyers in the nation, having advised hundreds of corporations and their shareholders and directors regarding the use of ESOPs in a wide variety of transactions, including leveraged buyouts, corporate stock repurchases, ownership succession transactions, and corporate reorganizations. He also regularly serves as legal counsel to ESOP trustees and lenders. Mr. Ackerman has provided legal counseling in connection with numerous large and complex ESOP transactions. This includes the recent $8.6 billion Tribune Company going-private transaction.

Mr. Ackerman is the immediate past chair of the ESOP Association's Advisory Committee Chairs' Council and is a past chair of the ESOP Association's National Legislative and Regulatory Advisory Committee. He has served on the board of directors of the ESOP Association. Mr. Ackerman is also an active member of the National Center for Employee Ownership and of Employee-Owned S Corporations of America.

Mr. Ackerman has lectured and written extensively on the subject of ESOPs. He is the author of over 20 published articles on the subject of ESOPs, including several articles published in the *Journal of Employee Ownership Law and Finance*. Mr. Ackerman speaks regularly at the annual national conferences of the ESOP Association and of the National Center for Employee Ownership and at their local and regional conferences. He has also made presentations regarding ESOPs at numerous other seminars, including programs sponsored by the American Institute of Certified Public Accountants and the American Society of Pension Actuaries; continuing legal education programs of several states, including Illinois, Minnesota, and Kentucky; and programs sponsored by the Illinois, Ohio, Michigan, and Heart of America chapters of the ESOP Association, the Ohio Employee

Ownership Center, the Chicago Bar Association, the Illinois CPA Society, and many banks and other financial institutions.

Mr. Ackerman received a J.D. from Harvard Law School in 1974 and a B.A. from Princeton University in 1971. He is admitted to practice in Illinois.

About the NCEO

The National Center for Employee Ownership (NCEO) is widely considered to be the leading authority in employee ownership in the U.S. and the world. Established in 1981 as a nonprofit information and membership organization, it now has over 3,000 members, including companies, professionals, unions, government officials, academics, and interested individuals. It is funded entirely through the work it does.

The NCEO's mission is to provide the most objective, reliable information possible about employee ownership at the most affordable price possible. As part of the NCEO's commitment to providing objective information, it does not lobby or provide ongoing consulting services. The NCEO publishes a variety of materials on employee ownership and participation, holds dozens of seminars, Webinars, and conferences on employee ownership annually, and offers a variety of online courses. The NCEO's work includes extensive contacts with the media, both through articles written for trade and professional publications and through interviews with reporters. It has written or edited several books for outside publishers. The NCEO maintains an extensive Web site at www.nceo.org.

See the following page for information on membership benefits and fees. To join, see the order form at the end of this section, visit our Web site at www.nceo.org, or telephone us at 510-208-1300.

Membership Benefits

NCEO members receive the following benefits:

- The bimonthly newsletter *Employee Ownership Report,* which covers ESOPs, equity compensation, and employee participation.
- Access to the members-only area of the NCEO's Web site, which includes a searchable newsletter archive, a discussion forum, a database of service providers, and more.

- Substantial discounts on publications, online courses, and events produced by the NCEO.
- Free access to live Webinars on ESOPs and related topics.
- The right to contact the NCEO for answers to general or specific questions regarding employee ownership.

An introductory NCEO membership costs $90 for one year ($100 outside the U.S.) and covers an entire company at all locations, a single professional offering services in this field, or a single individual with a business interest in employee ownership. Full-time students and faculty members who are not employed in the business sector may join at the academic rate of $40 for one year ($50 outside the U.S.).

Selected NCEO Publications

The NCEO offers a variety of publications on all aspects of employee ownership and participation. Below are some of our publications.

We publish new books and revise old ones on a yearly basis. To obtain the most current information on what we have available, visit us on the Web at www.nceo.org or call us at 510-208-1300.

Employee Stock Ownership Plans (ESOPs)

- *Understanding ESOPs* is an overview of the issues involved in establishing and operating an ESOP.

    $25 for NCEO members, $35 for nonmembers

- *Selling Your Business to an ESOP* is a guide for owners, managers, and advisors of closely held businesses, focusing on feasibility as well as on the tax-deferred Section 1042 "rollover."

    $25 for NCEO members, $35 for nonmembers

- *S Corporation ESOPs* introduces the reader to how ESOPs work and then discusses the legal, valuation, administrative, and other issues associated with S corporation ESOPs.

    $25 for NCEO members, $35 for nonmembers

- *Questions and Answers on the Duties of ESOP Fiduciaries* covers the legal issues relating to the nature and duties of ESOP fiduciaries in question-and-answer format.

    $25 for NCEO members, $35 for nonmembers

- *The Inside Fiduciary Handbook* provides an overview of the issues involved in being a fiduciary at an ESOP company.

    $25 for NCEO members, $35 for nonmembers

Equity Compensation

- *The Stock Options Book* is a straightforward, comprehensive overview covering the legal, accounting, regulatory, and design issues involved in implementing a stock option or stock purchase plan.

    $35 for NCEO members, $50 for nonmembers

- *The Decision-Maker's Guide to Equity Compensation* describes the various types of equity compensation, how they work, and how to decide much to give and to whom.

    $25 for NCEO members, $35 for nonmembers

- *Equity Alternatives: Restricted Stock, Performance Awards, Phantom Stock, SARs, and More* is a complete guide, including annotated model plans, to phantom stock, restricted stock, stock appreciation rights, performance awards, and more. A CD with plan documents is included.

    $35 for NCEO members, $50 for nonmembers

- *Equity Compensation for Limited Liability Companies* describes how equity compensation works in an LLC and provides a model plan document.

    $25 for NCEO members, $35 for nonmembers

To join the NCEO as a member or to order publications, use the order form on the following page, order online at www.nceo.org, or call us at 510-208-1300. If you join at the same time you order publications, you will receive the members-only publication discounts.

Order Form

This book is published by the National Center for Employee Ownership (NCEO). You can order additional copies online at our Web site, www.nceo.org; by telephoning the NCEO at 510-208-1300; by faxing this page to the NCEO at 510-272-9510; or by sending this page to the NCEO at 1736 Franklin Street, 8th Floor, Oakland, CA 94612. If you join as an NCEO member with this order, or are already an NCEO member, you will pay the discounted member price for any publications you order.

Name

Organization

Address

City, State, Zip (Country)

Telephone   Fax   Email

Method of Payment: ❏ Check (payable to "NCEO")   ❏ Visa   ❏ M/C   ❏ AMEX

Credit Card Number

Signature   Exp. Date

Checks are accepted only for orders from the U.S. and must be in U.S. currency.

Title	Qty.	Price	Total

Tax: California residents add 8.75% sales tax (on publications only, not membership)

Shipping: In the U.S., first publication $5, each add'l $1; elsewhere, we charge exact shipping costs to your credit card, plus a $10 handling surcharge; no shipping charges for membership

Introductory NCEO Membership: $90 for one year ($100 outside the U.S.)

Subtotal	$
Sales Tax	$
Shipping	$
Membership	$
TOTAL DUE	$